THE
Healing
Voice

Other books by
Joy Gardner-Gordon

Color and Crystals: A Journey Through the Chakras
Healing Yourself During Pregnancy
A Difficult Decision: A Compassionate Book About Abortion
The New Healing Yourself: Natural Remedies for Adults & Children
Our Earth Journey: A Journal Notebook

THE
Healing
Voice

Traditional & Contemporary
Toning, Chanting & Singing

Joy Gardner-Gordon

THE CROSSING PRESS
FREEDOM, CALIFORNIA 95019

Note to the Reader

The exercises described herein are given as information, and not as a prescription. They have not been tested on a broad sample of individuals, nor scientifically established. Therefore, neither the author nor the publisher can take responsibility for any positive or negative results which may be produced by using these exercises.

All the names of clients used in this book have been changed, and some are composites of actual clients, to protect their privacy.

Grateful acknowledgment is made for permission to reprint excerpts from previously published material:

Brown, Joseph Epes, *The Sacred Pipe: Black Elk's Account of the Seven Rites of the Oglala Sioux*, University of Oklahoma Press, Norman, Okla., © 1953.

Campbell, Don, *Music Physician for Times to Come, An Anthology.* Quest Books, Wheaton, Ill., 1991.

Lawlor, Robert, *Voices of the First Day—Awakening in the Aboriginal Dreamtone.* Inner Traditions, Rochester, Vt., 1991.

McGaa, Ed, excerpt from *Mother Earth Spirituality,* © 1990 by Ed McGaa, reprinted by permission of HarperCollins Publishers, New York, NY.

Powers, William K., *Yuwipi—Vision and Experience in Oglala Ritual.* University of Nebraska Press, Lincoln, Neb., 1982.

Powers, William K., *Sacred Language; The Nature of Supernatural Discourse in Lakota.* University of Oklahoma Press, Norman, Okla. 1986.

Copyright © 1993 Joy Gardner-Gordon
Book design by Amy Sibiga
Cover design by AnneMarie Arnold
Interior illustrations pp. 66, 68, 76, 113, 123, 131, 132, 141, 142, 150 by AnneMarie Arnold
Interior illustrations pp. 65, 92, 93, 94 by Amy Sibiga
Printed in the U.S.A.

Library of Congress Cataloging-in-Publication Data
Gardner-Gordon, Joy.
    The healing voice: traditional & contemporary toning, chanting & singing / Joy Gardner-Gordon.
      p. cm.
    Includes bibliographical references.
    ISBN 0-89594-571-1.--ISBN 0-89594-572-X
    1. Voice--Therapeutic use. 2. Singing--Therapeutic use.
    3. Chants--Therapeutic use. I. Title.
    RZ999.G313 1992
    615.8'51--dc20   92-36756
                                                  CIP

Acknowledgments

In her autobiography, *Blackberry Winter*, Margaret Mead noted the remarkable burst of creativity that emerges from women once they become clear that they will not bear any (more) children— whether that comes by simple choice or at the advent of meno- pause. Until that time, a woman's first priority is always her chil- dren, and so she must divide her loyalties.

This is my sixth book, and now that my children are grown, it is the first time that I have been able to totally throw myself into the creative process. I am just barely entering menopause, but since it has had such bad press, I want to acknowledge the joy it has brought me thus far.

I want to thank my husband, Gordon Raphael Gordon, who has brought me the rare and wonderful experience of unconditional love and support, and who has been a terrific and merciless editor.

This book would not have been written without the inspira- tion, encouragement and patience of my publishers, Elaine Goldman Gill and John Gill. I want to thank Arianna (Pamela) Nolan, Nick Mauro, and my editor, Claudia L'Amoreaux for reading and giving feedback on various versions of this manuscript.

I want to acknowledge Robert Lawlor, William K. Powers, Joseph Epes Brown and Pamela Amoss—authors who have acted as bridges to help others to understand the beauty and wisdom of people of other cultures. Thanks to all of the American Indians who have shared their lives with me, and particularly to Craig Carpen- ter, whose dedication to the Traditional way of life and to creating a bridge between his culture and mine has been a major contribu- tion to this book.

Finally, I want also to acknowledge the Muse, who has accom- panied me on every step of this exciting journey.

Joy Gardner-Gordon
Woodacre, California

I dedicate this book to all indigenous people of the world and to all people in the mineral, animal and plant kingdoms, in apology for the ignorance, the insensitivity, and the inability of "my people" to listen to your songs, to celebrate your cultures, and to learn from you. May this book be one of many sources that help to create a world in which we can all hear each other and sing together.

TABLE OF CONTENTS

Our task: chant the world.
Chant the beauty.
The world is a reflection of our chanting.

Billie Yellow
Navajo Healer

1

FINDING THE VOICE WITHIN

In virtually every culture throughout history, human beings have used toning, chanting and singing to praise their Creator and to heal their bodies and spirits. Our conventional Judeo-Christian culture is almost devoid of this healing tradition. Perhaps to fill this need, toning— the sustained, vibratory sounding of single tones, often vowel sounds, without the use of melody, rhythm or words—is quickly becoming a valuable tool for spiritually awakening people. Bypassing language entirely, toning allows us to express the heart and soul directly, quieting the over-active left brain.

When we give expression to the voice within, it emerges from the place deep inside that is at One with the Great Mystery, with God, with All and Everything. Inspiration is a word that describes both the intake of breath and receptivity to the Muse. When we truly touch that place within, we may become inspired to release that breath in words, tone, chant or song.

The human voice is one of our finest tools for healing the body and spirit. Yet it weighs nothing, it costs nothing, and you don't even have to carry it in your pocket. Toning has been practiced for eons by the Tibetans, Mongolians, Buddhists and Hindus. In one form or another, it is part of virtually every cultural tradition. Most people have heard the toning of the syllable OM, which is believed to create an energy of harmony and at-one-ness. Regardless of their religious training, people tend to move into an alpha state and experience a quiet centeredness when OM is toned repeatedly, especially if it is done by a person whose voice is rich and sonorous, or by a group of people.

The cry of an infant can be a form of toning. Infants are nonverbal, they are fully capable of expressing distress, happiness, love, and anger without words. Simply through the use of vibratory sound, they persuade us to pick them up, feed them, comfort them, or change their diapers.

When we learn to tone, it helps us reawaken the spontaneous and creative child within. It helps us tap into the pure "uncivilized" human being within, untouched by the stress of modern life. As we combine toning with other practices, we access the shaman or shamaness within— the one who speaks with spirits and heals with energy.

In this book I will describe traditional rituals which make use of toning, singing and chanting for healing and sacred purposes as they have been practiced by indigenous people before contact with the Europeans and Americans. I will explain how and why these rituals were suppressed by most organized religions and the governments they serve. Many of these rituals are now being revived, along with a new wave of interest in toning.

We are seeing a spontaneous emergence of the intuitive use of sounding (another word for toning). Almost every day I hear about new ways that people are using toning for spiritual expression, for enhancing community feeling, and for physical and emotional healing. People are listening to and expressing their inner voice in new and exciting ways: toning with Tai Chi, with yoga, with spontaneous dancing, with lovemaking; toning at men's groups, toning and wailing at women's groups.

If you wish to find the voice within, this book will be your guide. But first let us create a context within which to grasp the far-reaching effects of sound.

———————

Sound is the original mystical experience of creation: "In the beginning was the Word and the Word was God." The Sufi Master Hazrat Inayat Khan, who was both a great musician and a sage, commented on the Bible and other great works:

> We find in the Bible the words, "In the beginning was the Word, and the Word was God"; and we also find that the Word is Light, and that when that light dawned the whole creation manifested. These are not only religious verses; to the mystic or seer the deepest revelation is contained in them....
>
> It teaches that the first sign of life that manifested was the audible expression, or sound; that is the Word. When we compare this interpretation with the Vedanta philosophy, we find that the two are identical. All down the ages the Yogis and seers of India have worshipped the Word-God, or Sound-God; and around that idea is centered all the mysticism of sound or of utterance. Not alone among Hindus, but among the seers of the Semitic races too, the great importance of the word was recognized .... Sanskrit is now a language long dead, but in the meditations of the Indian Yogis, Sanskrit words are still used because of the power of sound and vibration they contain.[1]

The mystics of innumerable cultures agree upon the absolute power of sound. We begin with sound, we are held together by sound, and some day we will return again to the cosmic Music of the Spheres.

We do not live in a void. The so-called empty space around us is full of vibrations. We swim in a sea of sound waves and light waves and invisible units of electromagnetic energy pulsating continuously in every millimeter of space around us. We influence that space and are influenced by it. As long as we remain ignorant of our effect upon it and its effect upon us, we are merely spectators in a great drama that is being played in, around and through us.

Master Hazrat Inayat Khan gives us a scientific allegory of the power of the word:

> Scientists have discovered how radio messages can reach through space without any intermediary means ... Radio can explain to us ...

that no word once spoken is lost. It is there and it can be caught. This supports what is said above: that the sacred word has such power that nothing, whether distance, space, air or sea, can prevent it from entering and reaching the hearts that can catch it.[2]

Physics gives us another clue to understanding the power of sound. Physicists used to think that atoms were the smallest particles of matter in creation until it was found that an atom is composed of infinitesimal bits of matter moving in space. When physicists examined these bits of subatomic matter, they discovered they were not material at all, but just *energy vibrations* that appeared to be solid. "Quantum" is the name that was given to this infinitesimal unit of energy vibration. British physicist Stephen Hawking defines it as "the indivisible unit in which waves may be emitted or absorbed." Dr. Deepak Chopra coined the term "quantum healing."[3]

In his book, *Perfect Health, The Complete Mind/Body Guide*, he explains that the quantum field lies at the deepest level of the natural world. Dr. Chopra is a modern-day Western doctor who has been reviving the ancient Hindu practice of Ayurvedic medicine, which he learned originally from his grandmother.

According to Dr. Chopra, the sages of Ayurveda teach that primordial sounds are the threads that connect the universe. The body is held together by sound, and the presence of disease indicates that some sounds have gone out of tune.

Chopra explains that when two electrons are held together in a helium atom, an invisible but powerful bond holds them together despite distances that are greater, proportionally, than the distance separating the earth and the sun. Yet no Western scientist knows what this bond might be. Ayurveda teaches that primordial sound is the mysterious link that holds the universe together in a web that is the quantum field.[4]

The concept of primordial sound is not unique to Ayurveda. In *The Book of the Hopi* by Frank Waters, it says that "The living body of man and the living body of the earth were constructed in the same way. Through each ran an axis, man's axis being the backbone, the vertebral column, which controlled the equilibrium of his movements and his functions. Along this axis were several vibratory centers which echoed the primordial sound of life throughout the universe..."

The idea that there is a web of electromagnetic energy that holds the universe together is also echoed in the American Indian creation stories. The Creator Spirit of the Hopi is Grandmother Spider.[5] The Creator Spirit of the Lakota has no name, and his form is continuously changing, but he is known as Inktomi, the Spider, who is also the Trickster.[6] I have always puzzled over why the Indian people would designate a spider as the Creator.

As I have become aware of the invisible wave patterns that surround us, this invisible reality begins to resemble a spider web. I can almost see Grandmother Spider trapping an idea in her web, and weaving it into manifestation. In the ancient Aramaic language of the Bible, the word for "prayer" translates literally as "to set a trap."

The Word is the bridge between energy and material manifestation. Energy becomes sound and sound transports us into material reality. The spoken or sung word is the most powerful vibratory manifestor, which is one reason why radio and television are more powerful than the newspaper. Native people understand the power of using the voice—especially in song—to create and perpetuate the reality that they desire.

My Indian friend, Craig Carpenter, a semi-retired messenger for the Hopi Indians, says, "When we sing, we give thanks. And when we give thanks, then miracles begin to happen."

I know this to be true. My life has become a perpetual giving of thanks and I am constantly amazed by the "coincidences" and the "synchronicities" that unfold in my path. I hear the same from friends and students who take the time to meditate, and to give thanks for what they have—with words, with song, and with silence.

When we believe that we have no one to thank for our good fortune except ourselves; when we forget to sing and chant and give thanks for what we have; when we believe that we are totally separate individuals, living in a meaningless universe that has no connection with the Great Mystery or God or the cosmos; when we believe that our songs have no impact upon that universe, then our lives lose their mystery, and we forget about miracles.

It may be that when we continually praise life and give thanks for what we have—when we recognize, accept and express gratitude for our blessings—it enlivens the energy around us and makes us more potent manifestors, so that we can truly sing out and ask for what we need. Craig Carpenter puts it in simple terms:

> In case of emergency, us modern folks can run to the nearest
> telephone, take the receiver/transmitter off the hook, and punch a
> few buttons. Each one makes a different noise, and it goes by tones.
> If you're having a fire, a certain formula of tones will go to the local

fire station and they're supposed to come help you put the fire out. Or in case of an emergency regarding law enforcement, you touch a few tones and you get some guy with a gun on his hip. And if you're sick, you punch a bunch of buttons and get a different formula of tones and the ambulance will come screaming.

Well, old time traditional original way is, you just sing a few notes. That's all you have to do. Just holler. You just get that formula of notes and you can call on this particular angel or that particular angel—specialists, each one, in a particular gift of the holy spirit—a particular miracle gift.

And they come and investigate the situation. If they feel that you're worthy, or it's appropriate or necessary—putting out the fire, or healing the physical affliction, or the equivalent of police protection: bullet-proof, knife-proof, you name it—they've got it. Even for special insights, or wisdom, there are specialized angels with that gift, and you can call on them, too, with just a few notes.

And then—it just takes a sincere heart, actually, and a sincere wish or expression. You don't even have to say it in words sometimes. Then the Great Spirit of this Land and Life or his emissaries will come and hear your call for help and respond as appropriate. But how many people know that you can just sing a few notes, and there you've got it? Just holler.[7]

Could it be possible that the profound and virtually miraculous changes that have taken place in Russia and in Germany occurred in direct response to the worldwide call for peace that went out at the Harmonic Convergence on August 1989? At that time, hundreds of thousands of people all over the planet joined in silent meditation and the chanting of OM, in a heartfelt cry for peace.

As the ancients of virtually every culture believed, life begins with The Word. Through the breath and the word, we give our thoughts life. Through the vibratory power of the word and song, we enter the matrix of vibration from which all of life emerges. By changing our thinking, by remembering to be grateful for all that we have, and by giving voice to our inner song, it may be possible to increase our magnetism, to influence the earth's magnetism, and to create—to give rise to—miracles.

2

THE HOLOGRAPHIC SONG

To be inspired—with words, song, dance or art of any kind—is to breathe in, to swim in, to merge with the Muse. When you are truly inspired to sing, it's as if someone with an absolutely marvelous, powerful, perfect voice was singing through you. At the same time, it feels like this is the real you that has finally been set free and you are, at last, giving the performance of your lifetime—doing what you have always longed to do, becoming totally yourself.

Now how can that be? How can you be totally yourself, and totally not yourself at the same time? Holographic photography gives us a metaphor for how we can come from two entirely different perspectives at the same time.

An ordinary song is like a common two-dimensional photograph. You have a feeling, or you get an idea, and you sing about it. As in the photograph, one source of light hits the apple (the idea for the song) and then it strikes the photosensitive film, creating a reasonable facsimile of the apple—and thus you have the song.

Like the inspired song, the process of creating a three-dimensional image is more complex. We need to understand that light travels in wave patterns, and when these patterns intermingle, it's like throwing two pebbles into a pond at the same time; eventually the concentric circles run interference patterns with each other. To produce a holographic image of an apple, light is beamed through the laser into a beam splitter, which sends the light off into two separate directions. The first split beam will be bounced from the apple to a photographic plate. The second split beam will be deflected by one mirror and then another, and eventually sent to the same photographic plate where the two beams will meet and create minute interference patterns on the plate.

If you look at the film, all you will see are those concentric circle patterns that are superimposed on holographic photographs. Looking at the film plate with your naked eye, you will not see the image that has been photographed. However, if you pass a laser beam through the film, a three-dimensional image of the apple will appear. Unlike a normal two-dimensional photograph, you can actually walk around this image, and view it from any angle. [1]

Metaphorically, our bodies and our entire physical reality could be said to be produced when the original Light breaks off into two beams and then converges on the photographic plate of this planet, creating a maze of energy patterns that we interpret as our reality. But when we enter the trance state and become receptive to the Muse, as symbolized by the beam of laser light penetrating through the photograhic plate, then we enter another dimension as we bask in that light, and we become aware of the light of our True Self and the light of the Great Mystery, both interacting within us simultaneously, making us feel incredibly empowered and humbled at the same time. That is when we sing out a perfect song, which is our way of giving praise to the Divine Light.

This transcendent experience is so contrary to our normal way of life that the tendency is to (a) censor it and cut it off, (b) be embarrassed by it, (c) get big-headed about it, or (d) find a way to get rich with it. There is no other acceptable way to integrate such an experience into our "civilized" social fabric.

If we lived in a so-called "primitive" society, we could speak to the elders about our experience. They would understand it, and perhaps help us to interpret it and to integrate it into our lives, so that it might benefit others as well as ourselves. It might become part of a ritual that would allow us to re-live the transcendent experience, and to share it with the community.

I had the opportunity to experience my own holistic song during a ritual with the Apache Indians in New Mexico in 1967. I was living in the country near Taos when some of my white and Indian friends invited me to attend a meeting of the Native American Church, which was being held to bless their newly acquired land.

I heard that a Road Man (a holy man who conducts these all-night ceremonies) named Little Joe would be coming to their land from Taos Pueblo, and he wanted to be sure that there would be at least six people who "knew the songs" so they could "hold the energy." Our host reassured him that this would be taken care of.

When I arrived toward evening of the appointed day, the sun was already low on the horizon, painting the mesas in a brilliant salmon-colored wash. A tall, resplendent tepee graced the land. I could smell the fire as I went toward the group of Indian men who were wrapping something large in a white sheet. It was a whole young goat that had been skinned, and the Indian women were surrounding it with ears of unhusked corn. When the preparations were complete, the bundle was lowered into the pit over a bed of hot coals, and covered with dirt. They said it would cook throughout the night and then become part of the feast that would follow the ceremony.

Little Joe arrived with a couple of men from the Pueblo. He was a diminutive man who you would not notice in a crowd. I had seen that remarkable combination of humility and wisdom before, with Grandfather David of the Hopi and some Tibetan Lamas. He spoke with the Cedar Man, who would be tending the fire. As I recall, he walked quietly into the tepee and with his stick, he made an almost circular "road" in the sand around the fire pit at the center of the tepee. Then he rolled a Bull Durham cigarette (made from pure Virginia tobacco), took a few puffs, murmured something in his own language, put the cigarette out, placed it on the "road," and went out again. The Cedar Man went in and built the fire while people were arriving.

We all gathered outside the tepee—about twenty of us—and when the sun went down behind the mesa, Little Joe invited us in. Everyone was packed inside; we just barely fit around the circumference, crosslegged, with our knees scrunched up against each other. Little Joe was seated directly across from the entrance, facing East. Then the Cedar Man came in and closed the flap. He tended the fire, and we signaled him if we had to go out to pass water. We were asked not to fall asleep and not to leave the tepee for any other reason, because everyone who began the meeting should be there at the end of the meeting, to keep the energy together.

The Bull Durham was passed around the circle and we each rolled our own cigarette, took a few puffs, and placed our cigarettes on the "road." The ritual began with chanting. Little Joe muttered some prayers in Apache and the group broke into more chanting. Little Joe gave the drum to the man on his right and held onto the rattle. The person who holds the rattle is the one who speaks or sings while the person to the right accompanies on the drum.

This time Little Joe spoke in English. It was a long time ago, but I'll tell you how I remember it. "Hoh! Heavenly Father, Earthly Mother, thank you for this fire tonight and all these good people who've come to walk this road with us and bless this land. Thank you for this beautiful day today and all the women who came to help us cook. Thank you for this good path that you've given us to walk." He shook the rattle and the drummer took up the drum. The group broke into a lively chant.

Then Little Joe shook the rattle again and continued. "Great Spirit, I want to ask you to watch over my neighbor, Jim, 'cause he had a real bad accident two days ago when he fell off that combine and wrenched his shoulder. And his wife is havin' a hard time takin' care of him and the kids, too. HOH!" (He shook his rattle for emphasis, and several people said 'hoh' in agreement.)

Then he passed the rattle to George on his left. George was one of the men from Taos Pueblo. The drum was passed to Little Joe, so he could drum for George. There was a lot of chanting and then George said, "Hoh, Great Spirit, Father-Mother. We're travelling this road tonight, this good road that you have given to our people. We want to ask you to bless this land and take good care of Jake and Jim and Sandy and Inez, so there will be plenty of water, and the crops will grow tall, and there will be plenty of food to eat.

"And I want to ask you to help my mother, because that arthritis is getting pretty bad in her back and it's been hard for her to get out of bed these past few days. She wanted to be here tonight, but she just wasn't strong enough to make the trip. I want to ask you to comfort her and make that back strong again. HOH!" The rattle shook while other folks from the pueblo joined in the HOH in such a way that you knew they all knew his mother and cared about her and were sending her lots of good energy. Then they all broke out into a lively chant. The energy was already beginning to build.

Around midnight, a woman from outside brought a big pot of peyote tea to the entrance of the tepee. The Cedar Man received it and it got passed around. After we drank the tea, the energy picked up some more, the chanting intensified, and the prayers seemed more impassioned.

Never before had I heard ordinary people talking directly to God! Not only that—they were acknowledging the feminine aspect. I came from a culture where not even priests or rabbis talked to God. Where I came from, everyone in his or her right mind knew that only crazy people thought they could talk to God. But these people, whose lives had such direct simplicity, were teaching me something different.

As I listened to the drumming, chanting and praying, trying to avoid the smoke of the fire, my weariness built and it was difficult to resist lying down. I found myself almost sleeping in a sitting position, rocking back and forth in rhythm to the repetitive chanting.

There was something so familiar and comforting about the rocking movement and the deep chanting in a foreign tongue. The word *davvening* came to my mind. I felt myself being transported to a different place, a different time. I was a small child, being rocked in my mother's lap. It was Saturday, and we were at the sumptuous synagogue in Chicago. I have no doubt about the memories that ran through my mother's blood as she watched the rabbi *davvening* (rocking back and forth), in his white prayer shawl. Beside him was the cantor, who was also *davvening* with deep devotional emotion, chanting the sacred prayers in a language that I did not understand but loved to hear.

My mother must have been remembering the High Holy Days in their village in Poland, when all the neighbors came flocking to their home for the festivities. How exciting those special times must have been for her, watching her beloved father, who was both rabbi and cantor, with his great bushy beard and the *yarmulka* over his abundant black hair. Through her eyes, I can see him now, wrapped in his white prayer shawl, praying, *davvening*, chanting over the sacred prayerbook during the High Holy Days.

Those early experiences at Temple must have been my first awakening to spirituality. Margaret Mead said there are two ways to pass on spirituality to children: The first is for the mother to hold her child while she is having a spiritual experience. The second is to participate in rituals that are repeated again and again. Then the emotions and deep feelings that are experienced at one event will be recalled and brought up again when those rituals are repeated. I had the opportunity to feel that spiritual experience through my mother, and to experience it again every Saturday at services.

The rattle was being passed to the man on my right, and he was praying. This was the second time it had gone around the circle, and I knew it would be my turn soon. I had no idea what I would say. Through the night I had been listening to the Indian people chanting and praying aloud for their friends, their neighbors, their animals, their crops, for the boys in Vietnam, for the President of the United States, and for their parents. Suddenly it felt strange that I hadn't spoken to my parents in two years; I didn't even know where they were. My memories went back to my childhood.

I was eight years old when my family moved to Southern California and joined a new temple. I was shocked that there was no cantor, no one to chant the Hebrew prayers. I could not feel God in those services. They felt empty, shallow, devoid of spirit and passion. At the age of eight, I refused to go back to that synagogue. I felt confused and angry toward the women— especially my mother—who seemed to be there just to show off their new clothes. The temple suddenly felt like a superficial place, full of hypocrites pretending to be worshipping God.

So I turned my back on religion, and when I was an adolescent, I called myself an agnostic. But I was still looking for something. By the time I was thirteen, I was reading about Zen Buddhism and meditating. After a few years of meditation, I began to hear voices and see visions. Though I never met my grandfather (he was killed in the war by the Nazis), sometimes I had visions in which he would tell me personal things about himself. When I shared these stories with my mother, she confirmed that what he said to me was true, and in this way I knew that my experiences were real.

I left home in 1960, at the age of sixteen, and after a semester at the University of California at Berkeley, I adopted a way of life that came to be known as "hippie." Though my mother supported my spiritual quest, my parents were critical of the simplicity and poverty of my lifestyle. I moved to the Lower East Side in New York City, and became militantly judgmental of my parents' "conspicuous over-consumption." Sparks flew, and we disowned each other.

I must have been nodding out because I was startled when the man on my right began shaking the rattle. Everyone was chanting intently. My body rocked in rhythm to the chanting and suddenly I could hear my grandfather talking. It had been such a long time! He showed me an endless line of people—all related—holding hands, creating an unbroken linkage that benefits every member. Then I saw the place between myself and my mother. The link was broken.

My grandfather stood on the far side of my mother, holding her right hand with his left, while his own right hand linked up to a chain of relatives that seemed to stretch to infinity. My mother's left hand hung limp and useless at her side, while my right hand refused to take hers. I could feel that break of energy between us, and how much effort it took for me to reach my grandfather and my other kin as long as that link was broken.

Tears flowed down my cheeks and my heart felt full as the rattle was passed to me. The energy flowed from my heart to my throat as I broke into a wordless chant of wailing and toning that seemed like a combination of the Jewish High Holy Day songs and the Apache chants I'd been hearing all night. My soul poured out of my mouth as I expressed my grief, my sorrow and my longing for the connections that I did not have. When I was done, I shook the rattle fiercely and everyone shouted "HOH!"

At that moment, I was making my own mysterious and wonderful holographic connection, feeling simultaneously totally myself and totally connected to the Light.

After the meeting, I spoke with Little Joe, and he encouraged me to go back and find my parents. He also spoke about his concern about young people using drugs and peyote. I knew that Little Joe used peyote both as a sacrament and as medicine. He used it to pray, to open his consciousness to another level of reality and to bring that heightened awareness into his daily life. Many people had been healed of serious illnesses immediately after these meetings, and I later found out that George's mother was one of them. I understood that when we used the "medicine" as part of this ancient ritual, we were using it respectfully.

Perhaps the medicine helped us to focus as one energy so that when we asked with deep heartfelt emotion that someone we loved be healed, and particularly when everyone in the tepee joined their energies in that direction, the intent to heal became so strong that—if the person was ready to be healed—they could receive that positive vibration into their soul and use it to transmute the very cells of their body.

When I left Little Joe, I found my parents and mended the link with my mother, bridging that gap so that my children would know their grandparents and all the relations would be connected to one another. As I entered the world outside the tepee, I knew that I had had a direct experience of Spirit. I felt it when I was chanting.

3

RITUAL AND SONG

Throughout this book, various rituals are described which make considerable use of song. They are an arbitrary selection—not intended as a comprehensive survey. In the ceremonies in this chapter, the Lakota Sun Dancers pierce their flesh in a rite that closely resembles the ancient Australian Aborigines' circumcision ritual. The Aborigines seize the adolescent boys and keep them awake and without food until they go into a trance, much as the Coast Salish Indians "grab" a young man as part of his initiation as a Spirit Dancer. The feeling the Spirit Dancer describes when he is possessed by his song is almost exactly the same as the feeling of being possessed by the Holy Spirit at the Pentecostal Church meeting.

The continuity of rituals throughout this planet is uncanny. As we observe these rituals, it becomes apparent that they are not clever forms of entertainment, nor are they brilliant ideas that certain leaders devised for keeping people busy on Sundays. Every ritual described in this chapter has been practiced for more than one hundred years and was originally received as a visionary experience by holy people. All the songs and dances used in these rituals are believed to come from the same Source, and they are used to induce that same transcendent holographic experience.

According to Craig Carpenter, a messenger for various chiefs, spokes-men and traditional religious leaders, every Original Culture had a Spirit Being that appeared in temporary physical form and brought the people their Original Instructions. This includes Maasau for the Hopi, Buffalo Calf Woman for the Lakota, Wohpekahmau for the Pacific Coast Yurok and Jesus Christ for the Christians.[1] In every legend, these spirit beings ap-peared to holy people during particular visionary experiences.

This suggests that there is a common realm from which visions emerge, and that people of every culture have the ability to touch this realm. The method of entry often seems to be the trance experience, in which we leave behind the rational left brain and enter the intuitive realm, the abode of the Muse, the creative intelligence, the archetypal ancestral memories of the right brain—the Dreamtime, as the Australian Aborigines call it.

It doesn't seem to matter whether we enter this realm through the sensory deprivation that goes with the hunger and thirst of the Vision Quest, the self mutilation that goes with ceremonies like the Sun Dance, or the ritual use of mind-altering plants in the peyote and other ceremonies—*as long as it is done within a ritual, communal context.* Such experiences are almost always accompanied by some kind of song. Singing our prayers, our praise, our tones, our chants, helps to bring our consciousness into the alpha state wherein we touch the sacred realms.

There is a danger in living according to desiccated rituals that no longer have vitality for present times; most of our churches and temples are dying out because young people are drifting away. Our youth seem to prefer the quick glimpse into another reality that they get while on drugs, and yet they have no communal context in which to understand these exciting experiences and to assimilate them into their lives and the life of the community.

Young people need to be honored and their insights taken seriously. If we do not respect our youth, how can we expect them to give us the respect and love that elders have traditionally received? We need the insights of our youth, and a way of uniting their visions with our own, to constantly renew and recharge the fabric of our communities. They need our compassionate help to evaluate what they have experienced. Many of the young people on Indian reservations (and many of our own young people) are going back to the ancient rituals of the native Traditionalist elders, because these rituals fulfill their desire to be part of a meaningful, spiritual community.

We need rituals that are relevant to our current lives and opportunities to sing and dance and share our energies with a caring community. We need a context in which to have visionary experiences that will reconnect us with the realm of inspiration so that we can tap into the voice within, and find our own songs and dances, and our own truths.

When you sing a song repeatedly, the Lakota word is *piyalowan*, which is translated roughly, "to renew a song." An Indian doctor is *wapiye*, "someone who renews." The Lakota word for ceremony is *woapuje*: "to begin anew."[2] By understanding some of the ceremonies of the past, it may inspire us to seek the visionary experiences that will provide us with new rituals and new understandings of ourselves and of the people who observe some of these profound spiritual practices.

Vision Quest

This is a tradition common to many Indian tribes. It is one of the oldest rituals known to the Oglala, who refer to it as Crying for a Vision. A person goes into the regions of "wet and wildness" usually on top of a mountain, often in a place that is considered ritually sacred, a place of power. The supplicant may be naked, or have the minimal clothing and perhaps a blanket to sleep with, and no water or food.[3,4]

Before they go into isolation, they are expected to purify themselves. This means being clean in body, mind and spirit for several days before and after the ritual: not using foul language, not drinking alcohol, not having sexual intercourse. Their body should not smell of human contact, so they may be expected to bathe, to fast, and perhaps to take an enema.

The Sweat Lodge may be included in the preparation for the Vision Quest. It helps to quiet the heart and the mind and bring the participant into a more receptive frame of mind, thereby parting the veil between this world and the next. It is a valuable ritual in itself, as well as an excellent way to preceed other ceremonies. The Sweat Lodge is held in an igloo-shaped hut made of saplings covered with light, tightly woven blankets, with a fire pit at the center. People sit around the pit while red hot rocks that have been heated for hours in a bonfire are passed into the lodge on a shovel or similar device. A dipper of water is ritually sprinkled on the rocks, creating steam, which causes profuse sweating, like an intense sauna. This ritual is accompanied by prayers, good words and chanting.[5]

When it preceeds a Vision Quest, the Sweat Lodge may be ritually prepared by the elders, who may then accompany the supplicant to the questing place. Whoever oversees the Quest will probably return to check on him or her once every twenty-four hours. Crying for a Vision is considered potentially dangerous, and some people have been known to die, presumably because of encounters with evil spirits. When the proper rituals are observed, and when the supplicant is pure of heart, it is believed that his or her own spirit helpers will provide protection. William K. Powers spent many years living among the Lakota, and he seems to have been well regarded by them. He gives this description of the dramatic visions that have been seen by some vision questers:

> The idea of the Wakinyan, or "Thunder Beings", approaching the supplicant on the Vision Quest by means of a road built alongside the clouds is common among the Oglala. The supplicant is instructed to expect a phenomenon such as this. He is told that if he keeps looking at the clouds soon they will open up and he will see the Wakinyan Oyate "Thunder People" coming toward him. He should not be afraid. There will be many of the thunder people each riding a horse and driving a slave before him. They will be coming toward the supplicant in great numbers, but all he has to do is point the sacred pipe at them and they will pass him by.[6]

The area is staked out in some way, perhaps with prayer flags or by digging a hole for the vision quester to stay in. The supplicant has no weapons and is expected to stay in this one place, enduring several days and nights of boredom combined with the deprivation of food and water, constantly praying and chanting aloud, humbling his or herself before the spirits, overcoming his or her fear, asking to be a vehicle to receive the vision or the visitation from a spirit helper. Whatever occurs on the mountaintop is considered significant, particularly the appearance of birds, animals or insects, and the occurrence of dreams or visions.

During this time of isolation, the supplicant might go to the four directions, to offer the pipe and "lament." The Lakota word for "to pray," *cekiya* is derived from *ceya*, "to cry, to lament," and the inserted preposition *ki* means "for." From an Indian perspective, prayer and a kind of toning are one and the same thing, as though you could not speak to the Great Spirit in a normal tone of voice, but would have to sing, cry, tone, wail, or speak in the ancient sacred language in order to make yourself heard. Powers comments:

> In all cultures of the world, it is as if exaltation of the supreme deity and propitiation of the supernaturals are somehow made stronger, clearer, more determined if sung rather than spoken in common prayer. Frequently, people feel more secure, more assured, somehow more satisfied if they can sing out their innermost feelings and sentiments rather than simply utter them in the monotonous register of prayer.[7]

Black Elk, an Oglala (a branch of the Lakota) Holy Man, told Joseph Epes Brown about the Vision Quest:

> There are many reasons for going to a lonely mountaintop to 'lament.' Some young men receive a vision when they are very young and when they do not expect it, and then they go to 'lament' that they might understand it better. Then we 'lament' if we wish to make ourselves brave for a great ordeal such as the Sun dance or to prepare for going on the warpath. Some people 'lament' in order to ask some favor of the Great Spirit, such as curing a sick relative; and then we also 'lament' as an act of thanksgiving for some great gift which the Great Spirit may have given to us. But perhaps the most important reason for 'lamenting' is that it helps us to realize our oneness with all things, to know that all things are our relatives; and then in behalf of all things we pray to *Wakan-Tanka* that He may give to us knowledge of Him who is the source of all things, yet greater than all things.
>
> Our women also "lament," after first purifying themselves in the *Inipi*; they are helped by other women, but they do not go up on a very high and lonely mountain. They go up on a hill in a valley, for they are women and need protection.[8]

Various tribes report that women have spontaneous visions at the time of their period, or during childbirth. Since the Oglala women were not allowed to go to the strongest power spots, their visions were usually weaker than the men's, and so they did not often become powerful shamans.[9]

Yuwipi

Yuwipi is a mystical Lakota healing ritual that is over 150 years old. It was born out of a Vision Quest experience over 150 years ago when Horn Chips was a little boy. Both his parents had died, and he lived with his grandmother. The other children made so much fun of him that he decided to end his life. Then he heard a voice that told him he would grow up to be a great man, and the voice instructed him to go up to a high mountain, dig a hole four feet deep and stay there without food or water for four days. Horn Chips did as he was told, and he had a vision in which a snake came to him and gave him instructions on how to conduct the Yuwipi healing ceremony.

The Yuwipi man is like a combination high priest, medium and shamanic healer. The people call him *Tunkasila*, "grandfather," a term of great respect. He may call himself *iyeska*, "interpreter" or "medium," because he alone can understand the spirits that speak to him during the ceremony, and he has a responsibility to the spirits to communicate their messages back to the people.

Yuwipi men are not supposed to charge for their services, but if a person benefits from the ritual, he or she will be expected to make a gift, and in the Lakota tradition, that person and their family will be expected to sponsor a thanksgiving ritual within a year. If this is not done, it is believed that it will anger the spirits, and the person who was helped will be in danger.

Traditionally, the individual who is sick will approach the Yuwipi man for healing. In the old days, a relative or close friend of the sick person would offer to do a Vision Quest while the Yuwipi ceremony was being held. The one who was Crying for a Vision would further his own spiritual evolution, while "helping out" the one who was ill. That doesn't seem to be a part of contemporary Yuwipi ceremonies.

The Lakota use the word "meeting" when referring to a Yuwipi in English, but the Lakota word, *lowanpi*, translates as "sing," because there is lots of singing in this ritual. Each Yuwipi man, or leader of the ceremony, receives his own unique songs for the ritual from the spirits, and these he teaches to the lead singer or singers. The songs are repetitious, with just a few lines to each chant, so everyone who attends the meeting is encouraged to join in and "help out."[10]

There are few Yuwipi men still in existence, but *New Age Journal* ran an article in July/August 1992 about Horn Chips's great-grandson, Godfrey Chips, now in his thirties, who is the fourth in a long line of Yuwipi men. He has been doing ceremonies since he was thirteen, when the spirits came and spoke to him for three months. He is the first to do ceremonies for non-native people, because in 1985 the spirits came and told him, "The pipe belongs to everyone."[11]

The room for the Yuwipi ceremony is totally gutted of all furniture and all signs of civilization, which are considered offensive to the spirits. The windows are hung with black plastic to block out any possible light. The main singers sit against the west wall, looking toward the doorway which faces east. William K. Powers gives a dramatic description of the Yuwipi that he attended, which was led by Plenty Wolf.

> The kerosene lamp remained lit on the floor near the doorway. Its tiny flame flickered, washing the somber faces of the adepts with a yellow ochre glow. Thirty people had assembled, and only they and the sacred altar were highlighted; the rest of the room gave up its discernible shape to the blackness. Sacred time had not yet arrived, and a few still whispered and joked; a baby sucked noisily at a nursing bottle filled with soda pop. A singer finally tapped his drum impatiently, waiting for the sing to begin. This is characteristic of singers at sacred as well as secular events. They are very much aware that no ceremony can begin without them, and once they have arrived little time elapses before they make their presence known, usually by testing the drum. The signal was taken seriously by the adepts, who immediately became solemn, squirming into more comfortable positions around the periphery of the room.[12]

The ceremony began with the Yuwipi man lighting the sacred pipe and praying to the seven directions: the Four Winds, the Above, the Earth, and the Spotted Eagle, who is sacred to Wakantanka. Then he prayed in the sacred language. At that point the singers came in with the first song, in a whining, crying high falsetto. The introduction quickly segued into a second song that was done in a yelping fashion. [13]

Then the Yuwipi man was covered with his own blanket and bound tightly with leather thongs, like a mummy, and placed face down in a bed of sage at the center of the room. The room was totally darkened.

> As the singers began the next song, their voices were interrupted by the clatter of rattles striking the floor and walls of the darkened room.... The singers continued unperturbed, their voices stronger, their words clearer.[14]

The Yuwipi man prayed for those who were ill, and those who wished to be cured stood up in the dark while the singers continued their loud singing and drumming. A first-hand account of this experience is given by Mary Louise Dow, who sought out Godfrey Chips during a Yuwipi Ceremony in Massachusetts, to help heal a cancerous tumor that was too large for the doctors to remove. He told her to come to a ceremony at his home in Pine Ridge, South Dakota. She describes her experience in *New Age Journal*.

> Suddenly I heard amid the deafening voices a loud thud, like two heavy footfalls. It was as if someone had jumped down to the floor from the ceiling or roof. But if you could see this rickety old structure you'd know that was not possible. Before I could think any more about the noise, I saw something rise amid the darkness, something blue and luminous. It appeared to be the sacred gourd that had been placed on the altar in front of Godfrey....The gourd was moving around the room, pulsating blue light whenever it moved or shook. Like with the unseen feather I had felt in the ceremony in Massachusetts, I could neither see nor feel anyone around me as I watched the gourd—even after the little blue lights began moving around my abdominal area [where the cancer was].

After another chant, the lights were turned on and the Yuwipi man was sitting at the center of the room, the leather thongs rolled into a neat little ball. The ceremony was complete.

There are many stories of miraculous healings following Yuwipis. After Mary Louise Dow returned to her doctor in California, she had this story to tell:

> "This really is amazing," my chemo-oncologist was telling me as I lay in a hospital bed a month after returning East from Pine Ridge. I had just undergone successful surgery, and the doctor and I were reviewing my medical records. My tumor originally had been considered unexcisable because it was the size of a grapefruit, he told me, but by the time it was surgically removed it had been reduced to the size of a lemon. My case, I later would learn, also was making the rounds at the hospital where the surgery was performed; the doctors there were saying that the shrinkage in my tumor was remarkable. Even my surgeon, whom I had come to know as a quiet man of few words, was speaking to me with newfound encouragement about my prognosis. [15]

Sun Dance

The vision that led to the Sun Dance was received by Kablaya, a Holy Man of the Lakotas. As he was instructed, he gathered all the neighboring tribes to participate in the ritual. He told them that a cottonwood tree should be ceremonially selected, blessed, cut down and brought to the center of the dance area. He taught the songs to the singers, and told them to bring a large round drum made from a buffalo hide, and strong drum sticks, covered at the ends with buffalo hide.

The ceremony began with singing and dancing just as the sun came over the horizon. The singers were required to sing all day without respite, to hold the tension for the dancers. As the singers and drummers increased their speed, the helpers grabbed Kablaya and threw him on the ground. The helper pulled up the skin of Kablaya's breast and pierced it with a sharpened stick. A leather thong that hung from the tree was fastened to the stick. They stood Kablaya up and he blew on his eagle-bone whistle as he leaned back on his thong and danced. Then the other men did the same.

The men, and some women, danced in the hot sun, without food or water, until the thongs tore open their flesh. Just before sundown a pipe was brought to the singers and drummers so they could stop and smoke. Later there was a great feast and much rejoicing, for the people felt that a great thing had been done, and the Lakota Nation would be strengthened by this ceremony.[16]

Circumcision Ceremony of the Australian Aborigines

The Sun Dancer's piercing of the flesh is not unlike the circumcision ceremony that has been practiced by the Australian Aborigines for over 100,000 years. Several boys are taken into the jungle and decorated with blood from the veins of the older men, to symbolize a new birth in consciousness. They are deprived of food and not allowed to speak. They are kept awake all night for several nights, constantly in the presence of repetitive singing and dancing, until they enter into a trance. Then the older men instruct them, in chant and song, about the ancient laws and truths and legends.

When the seizure ends, they are carried like corpses back to camp, to the wailing women (their role in this drama is carefully choreographed) who will mourn over the loss of their babies and feed the young men. Then they are taken on a ceremonial journey away from the village where they will meet some of their distant kin from other camps who will join them and return to the boy's camp to participate in the circumcision rite.

The ceremonial ground is set like a stage in a complex drama, with the entire clan or village taking part. Though the operation is a painful one, the initiation process has taught the boy how to enter a trance state so that he will not feel the pain.

> The young novice is led into the center of the ceremonial ground amid groups of grievously crying women, fiercely painted dancers, and blazing fires. At a moment of crescendo, a group of performing men rush toward the central fire and, bending over in front of it, form a human platform or table on which the boy is laid. The relative who is to perform the cutting leaps up and sits on the boy's chest, facing his penis and the conflagration.... The operator cuts the foreskin with a sharp quartz tool, while the grandfather, circling the human altar, continually reassures the boy....
>
> The ceremonial ground rises to a frenzy of dancing, singing, and moaning, accompanied by the wild hum of bullroarers (wooden rods with lashes fastened to them that, when twirled, produce a low, humming sound).

For several days the boys remain in seclusion, and they are not allowed to speak, except by sign language. The all-night dance ceremonies continue while the old men instruct the boys about the nature of the journey they must make after death. When the young men return to the community, they have ended their period of dependence upon their mother, and they have been initiated into their sacred responsibility toward the earth, the Universal Feminine.[17]

Coast Salish Spirit Dancing

It is uncanny how similar the Aborigine Circumcision Ceremony is to the "grabbing" of reluctant candidates for the Spirit Dance. The traditional Spirit Dance is still practiced by about 20% of the Nooksack Coast Salish Indians of northwestern Washington. They say that they become "possessed" by a song, *syowen*, that comes to them and demands to be expressed. In the old days, the *syowen* would usually come during a Vision Quest, but these days no one goes out questing because all their sacred places have been "polluted by human use."

A person is most likely to experience a vision when he is in a highly susceptible condition, which could occur during a fever, or while grieving over the death or loss of a loved one, or even from extreme anger toward a lover, parent or child. The person might weep continually until his or her cries turn into the characteristic groans of a Spirit Dancer. At such times, it is said that "the *syowen* 'takes pity on' the unhappy person."

According to Pamela Amoss, in her book, *Coast Salish Spirit Dancing, The Survival of an Ancestral Religion,* "the participants usually attribute their own decision to become dancers to forces beyond their control. In the native view, people become dancers because they have to, not because they want to."

Another reason for becoming a Spirit Dancer is to heal illness.

> People love to tell about friends or relatives stricken with cancer or some other dread disease who, having been dismissed by the white doctors, were saved by initiation as spirit dancers. Furthermore, the strength of an Indian dancer is believed to protect him from all kinds of sickness and accidents and to see him through to a ripe old age.[18]

The whole social, moral and ethical fabric of indigenous society is maintained through a complex kinship system, with its duties toward both living and dead relatives. The deceased are known to cause trouble if they are unhappy, so many of the rituals are designed to propitiate the dead. Sometimes the spirit helper of a dead ancestor will want to come into a living relative. A person who resists may become weak and sickly, and an Indian doctor will recognize when the problem is caused by the *syowen.* The doctor can lift the spirit off temporarily, but after three or four times, "If her spirit bothers her again next year, she will just have to yield to the inevitable and become a dancer."

"Grabbing" is one of the most popular ways of getting new members these days. A family might set up a youth to be grabbed because of a drinking problem, or because of difficult and rebellious behavior. It is an interesting alternative to our society's threat of jail. The boy or girl has to be at least semi-willing to be grabbed, and the family has to be fully willing.

> It is not possible, however, for a person to enjoy a socially approved relationship with spiritual beings without the support of kinsmen. Without family help he cannot arrange the gatherings, the payments, and the peripheral expenses that are the necessary parts of social validation of his supernatural connection.[19]

When a candidate is chosen, a number of men from the dancing community will literally grab the young person and lift him or her up and carry the person away, keeping the young person awake and isolated for a prolonged period in a condition of sensory deprivation combined with singing and drumming, until the weary candidate falls into a trance. Then the person will tend to have visions, usually of an animal spirit helper. The person's power and their song will come from this helper.

The Spirit Dance takes place many times and in many locations during the winter season. Each dancer performs his or her own unique dance and song. When singers go into a trance, they may begin by crying, groaning or sighing. They report feeling a pain in their chest or a feeling of heaviness. Some hear their song before they begin singing.

> At the very time when the dancer is deeply entranced and most isolated from other people he is most closely tied to the Indian community and most wholeheartedly supported by it. When a person dances, the other people present gather around him to help him. They sing and drum for him. They protect him from the dangers of evil supernatural forces by the screen their bodies form around him. They pour their own feelings into the singing of his song....

When the song comes through, the dancer experiences release and fulfillment: "When the drumming is right, it feels like floating!" "When I start to jump around, I don't feel nothing." After the dancing, community feeling is warm and close, especially in small groups.[20]

Speaking in Tongues

The Pentecostal Church became popular among the Coast Salish and other Indians, because it so nearly resembled their own trance experiences. In the mainstream of Christianity, possession by the Holy Spirit is considered all right for the old saints and prophets, but not for the masses.

At the Pentecostal and Baptist Churches, possession is condoned when it is expressed through speaking in tongues, which possesses the person in a way that is very similar to the *syowen* possession. This experience is described by a woman who was a member of the Pentecostal Church as a child in Southern California:

> After the sermon, the Minister would pray for the sinners and give them a chance to come down and be saved—to submit themselves to Christ. The whole church would be in a meditation-type place where they'd all be praying. I'd close my eyes, and the prayer

would seem to go on forever. I could hear through the church that people were more or less talking under their breath and saying things like "Dear Jesus!" and giving praise to God, and telling Him how good He is, and thankful and hallelujah.

And if you felt called then you could walk down the aisle to the front, to the altar and get down on your knees and let everybody witness the fact that you are giving your heart to Jesus. And there might be other people up there at the same time. So while you're down on your knees praying for your sins, of course you're crying; it gets very very emotional. All the things you've done wrong are coming up and out.

And when you do that, the church leaders will come down and lay their hands on you and pray for you. And it just seems that the energy is so great; it's just an incredible feeling. I remember when I did that and we had a visiting minister and he laid hands on me and I went under the power of the Holy Ghost. I fell totally backwards, almost in a faint. I guess people helped me down, because I just went backwards and I was just layin' there mumbling. And then I just came up with this verbiage that I could hear in one realm, but in the other, I wasn't a part of it. I just didn't have control over my tongue.

So that's when you're making all the sounds, and talking in tongues. It never really sounded like another language. I can't even do it. I can't mimic it. There were a lot of rolls, a lot of la-la-la-la. But you do repetitively use the same syllables again and again to get into the power of it. It has a certain lilt to it. It's a song without a lot of ups and downs.

When it's over, it just naturally goes into "Oh Jesus, thank you God." You do feel like you've been close to God. And once you do that, there is a complete lightening up of your burdens. It feels like you have no cares, because now they are in God's hands. Then thereafter, when you pray after church services, it just comes out again.[21]

All of these rituals are true spiritual experiences, in which the participants actually touch the spirit realms with the assistance of toning, chanting and singing. They are not empty rituals, nor are they likely to be works of magic or trickery. The results may be miraculous healings, but the deeper purpose is expressed in the most beloved song of the Sun Dancers:

Wakantanka pity me.
I want to live; that's why I am doing this.[22]

The ultimate healing is to go into the vision, the trance, the Dreamtime, and to make it so much a part of our lives that we understand, along with the Australian Aborigine, that

> Neither the dream nor the phenomenal world is considered an illusion; rather, together they constitute reality. [23]

4

ORAL HISTORIES AND A MIRACLE STORY

For thousands of years the people of this planet have had their histories literally pounded into their heads by the rhyme and rhythm of songs and dances, by bards and minstrels, by poets and storytellers, through ancient chants and prayers. Through this "primitive" system, people could compare histories not only through the use of the spoken word but also through the medium of songs and dances.

Like most modern-day Westerners, I assumed that oral history was a poor substitute for written history, that it was a tradition that died out long ago. In fact, the change to written history occurred—on a large scale—only about 200 years ago, with the widespread use of the printing press.

Oral histories are still being preserved by the Hopi, the Australian Aborigines, and other Traditional people who—to this day—have no written language. The Aborigines refused writing, just as they refused clothing and buildings, because they are not a part of their instructions from the Dreamtime.[1]

In south India, there are sacred families whose main work is the chanting of the sacred scriptures; sometimes a priest will concentrate exclusively on one epic. Bhagvatar is a priest who is well known for his chanting of the *Ramayana*, an epic poem of 24,000 verses. The recital of the *Ramayana* requires twenty-four performances of four hours each. That is the equivalent of twelve eight-hour days!

In the *Mahabharata*, another epic poem, Arjun is a warrior, musician and dancer. His charioteer is the god Krishna, who gives basic guidelines for right action and justice in the heat of battle in the famous *Bhagavad Gita*, the Song Divine. *Gita* means song, and it is like the bible to the Hindus.[2] Can you imagine memorizing the entire bible?

In seeking an understanding about how such phenomenal feats of memorization and attention to detail were accomplished, I came upon this excerpt from James Mooney, a noted anthropologist, who visited the Paiute Holy Man Wovoka in 1891 and observed the following interaction:

> Each statement by the older man was repeated at its close, word by word and sentence by sentence, by the other, with the same monotonous inflection. This done, the first speaker signified by a grunt of approval that it had been correctly repeated, and then proceeded with the next statement, which was duly repeated in like manner.[3]

The "monotonous" hypnotic inflection is used by many cultures when chanting the ancient teachings. This is seen in the oral tradition of the Jewish scholars. Although the words are written, Yehuda Landsman tells how these scholars study the holy *Talmud*:

> If you walked into a Yeshiva (a school for young adults for learning the Talmud), you would hear people chanting their learn-ing. When you read the Talmud, you're supposed to do it out loud, and in a certain rhythm. So it's quite a noisy place. Even two people

talking together and getting excited about some fine point in the Talmud are likely to break into chanting their words. I think the chanting enhances that *alpha* state. Because the Torah, remember, isn't just old knowledge that you're studying—it's a living knowledge that's constantly evolving, and people are encouraged to find their own ideas. I think that by attaining an *alpha* state through the chanting, it provides space for new inspirations to come through.[4]

The same theme recurs among the Australian Aborigines, where grandparents kept the little ones entertained with simple versions of the myths that were part of their culture. These stories might be told as songs, dances, or even sign language. [5]

Similarly, in ancient Hawaii, the firstborn child would become the constant companion of the grandparents, "listening, learning, rehearsing, so even the tempo and cadence of *pule* (prayers) and *oli* (chant) would be traditionally correct."[6]

Perhaps the firstborn child would grow up loving to play with words and rhythms and would become a *haku mele*, a poet. This term derives from *haku*, which is the sorting out of feathers and arranging them in patterns for feather cloaks and other decorations, and *mele* which means song, chant or poem. Chants were used for virtually every occasion. A chant would be given to honor the firstborn of the senior line of a family. Babies of nobility would be given a birth song which would describe the mother's pregnancy and childbirth as well as the cosmological and astrological circumstances of the birth.

The Hawaiian nobility had chants that recorded the events that were significant to the family history: battles, travels, building of *heiau* (outdoor temples), and natural phenomena such as volcanoes and tidal waves. There were chants about voyages and creation chants. There were complex rituals and chants to honor the gods. All of these chants were considered powerful, *mana*, and ritually sacred, *kapu*.

There is a great deal of ritual importance attached to Polynesian genealogy, especially for nobility who reputedly can trace their ancestry back to the gods, and even to the beginning of life in the universe. These genealogy chants would be reserved for ceremonial occasions—births, deaths, certain rituals, and when they were required to establish a line of power.

The composition of the longer, more formal poems would typically require a group convened by a chief or a royal *haku mele*. Such a group would follow a specific procedure in composing a *mele*. A line would be proposed, then it would be criticized and evaluated. When the line was approved by the group, one of the poets was asked to memorize it. At the end of the day all the lines they had composed were recited and everyone in the group memorized the entire composition. By the time the chant was completed—even if it took many days—each bard had committed the entire chant to memory. In this way, poets became the historians and recordkeepers of the court.[7]

Polynesian religions were marked by a hierarchy of gods usually headed by four principals. In Hawaii they were named Kane, Ku, Lono, and Kanaloa. Their collective name is *akua*. Each lesser god is linked to the family of one of these four gods. The help of the major gods was invoked for major causes and great events. Their worship demanded great attention to detail, knowledge and organization of ritual. Unlike the *aumakua*, the family and personal gods, the major gods were not considered approachable by the common people.

The elaborate rituals of Kane and Ku lasted for days in specially consecrated *heiaus* (structures of worship) with hosts of *kahunas* (priests). Only the *kahunas* knew the proper ritual chants and could appeal to the major gods on behalf of the nobility and commoners. [7, 8]

I gained more appreciation for the Hawaiian *kahunas* from my Indian friend, Craig Carpenter. For thirteen years, Craig was one of the most active messengers for the Hopi Independent Nation. He worked for and between various chiefs, spokesmen and Traditional and religious leaders (primarily Hopi). He told me the following story about his first meeting with Master Kahuna David Kaonohiokala Bray ("Daddy Bray") in 1957. I asked permission to record Craig's story, and he agreed.

Craig was working as a part-time printer for a publishing company in Los Angeles that put out metaphysical books, including one well-known book about Hawaiian kahunas. A friend of the publisher knew Daddy Bray, and said that he had some information that contradicted what was in their book. So he brought Daddy Bray to meet the publisher, and that's where Craig's story begins.

I will give the story here, almost as he told it, so you can appreciate his uncanny memory and attention to detail. I have had to cut out at least half of the narrative, and a great deal of his meticulous detail, both to protect the privacy of others and for the sake of brevity. This story will clearly illustrate the historic power of traditional songs and the strength of the oral tradition.

As Craig began his long narration, his eyes turned inward and his voice took on a sing-song, chanting rhythm, without much variety or inflection, as though he were a messenger bringing news from afar, concentrating deeply to be certain that no mistakes were made.

I was working at the printing press when the front door tinkled. I looked up and in walked this little brown man with white hair. On one side of him was a gigantic white man who was so tall he had to stoop to come in the door. On the other side was a normal-sized white man.

I thought I knew all the Hopis in Los Angeles. "Who's this guy?" I thought to myself. He sure looked like a Hopi to me. The tall white man came in and asked for Wing Anderson.

Wing came out of his inner office, set a circle of chairs, started visiting with him, and hollered back at me, "Craig, stop the printing press, you've gotta hear this."

And Daddy Bray told a story: he was living in a hotel room in Honolulu. He woke up early one morning, maybe two o'clock or so. There was a fire right in the middle of the the rug. He thought the hotel was on fire. When he finally got his thoughts collected, the voice of the Goddess Pele [the Hawaiian goddess of the volcano] came out of the fire and told him to go to the Mainland and investigate a religious rebirth that was taking place here.

So Daddy Bray came to the Mainland, and stayed with some friends who had a well known printing firm in San Francisco. They introduced him around to their friends. He investigated and inquired, but he didn't find any religious rebirth. He kept looking but he couldn't find any. So finally when there were only a few days left of his tour or his vacation, he figured he better visit his two daughters.

One was in Reseda, the other was in San Diego. Daddy Bray was staying with his daughter Odetta in Reseda at the time I met him.

"But," he said, "I've been here in Los Angeles. I've looked around for a religious rebirth, and all I can find is a bunch of religious cranks. I don't know what I was sent over here for, but I do know I don't belong here, and in four days I'm going back home to the islands again."

So then he turned to me, and he asked me those four questions that Hopis ask of high-class people. Not that I was a high-class person, but I had some information. He asked me (1) where I was from, (2) what my name was, (3) what my religion was, and (4) why I was there, in Los Angeles.

In the course of answering those questions, I had a chance to bring out a brief review of the Hopi Message of Peace, which tells (1) where we as human beings came from (the underworld that was destroyed at the last great cleansing or purifying of wickedness off the face of the earth), (2) why we came to this land, (3) what happened to us after we came here (how we met the Great Spirit and received His permission to live in this land with Him, provided we followed certain specific instructions as to our way of life and our religious practices), (4) what is happening to us now (the period at the end of this long era in which we're being tested and tried to see if we can remain faithful to our original instructions, no matter what happens to us)—and then the last point (the fifth finger of the hand), (5) what may happen to us and all the life forms on this earth if we as human beings do not correct ourselves and our leaders in accordance with our own original instructions while we still have time—if we want to.

So I gave him the five basic points of the Hopi Message of Peace, and then turned to him and asked if he had any prophesies at all similar to these. His eyes got big and he said, "We sure have!" He excitedly asked, "Can we excuse ourselves and talk about these matters in greater detail?"

So we did. And while the other three men talked over old times and renewed their close ties, Daddy and I went off to one side and talked more and more. He'd ask me questions. I'd try to give him more details on what I'd already told him, explaining all the while that I was just a messenger; I wasn't a leader, and if he wanted to get it exactly right, he had to go talk to those Hopi leaders and get it from them face to face.

Daddy Bray asked Craig to call him the next day at his daughter's house so they could get together for dinner and talk some more. That evening Craig got a call from Bob Luteweiler, a well-known Quaker who was doing a tour of intentional communities. He planned to go to Hopiland and he wanted the names of some Hopi leaders. Craig offered to go with him to introduce him personally, and asked if he had room for two passengers. He did. The next day Craig phoned Daddy Bray to tell him they had a ride to Hopiland, and did he want to go?

Daddy said, "Oh, do I! But wait a minute. Let me have a chance to be quiet, will you? I'll phone you back in a couple hours, okay?"

I said, "Fine."

So he phoned back in half an hour—not a couple of hours. And he said, "Do you know what they tell me? They tell me this is the religious rebirth I was supposed to investigate, over in North America," he says. "In all my years in Hawaii, I never met another Indian. I certainly never heard of Hopis before. How'd the Goddess Pele know what's going on in Hopiland? I want to go talk to those Hopi leaders."

Then he says, "But—since I represent a high-class family from Hawaii, I have to go in a traditional way, and that means I have to send a messenger ahead of me, one day, to let the Hopi leaders know I'm coming so they can prepare for me. Is that all right with you?"

I said, "Yes, of course."

He said, "I've already phoned my son-in-law in San Diego. He's a forest ranger. He knows how to travel the back country. So you tell him the directions and who to ask for when we get there, and we'll figure on it. You go ahead with Bob Luteweiler and I'll come out the day after."

So I said, "Fine." Then I talked to the son-in-law, the forest ranger, and told him what he needed to know. And all was well. I then told Bob what had happened and we jumped in the car and took off. I did introduce this famous Quaker around to the proper leaders, and while he was visiting with them, I'd tell other leaders, "Hey, this Hawaiian is coming. He may be the biggest *poakka* in the world, I don't know, but he's got *power*. He says he's going to follow me in one day. Maybe he will, maybe he won't." (A *poakka* in Hopi language is a "two-heart," a magician who is sometimes evil because the magician desires both good *and* evil.)

"His name is Daddy Bray," I told them. "He was being raised by his Grand Aunt in the court etiquette of traditional Hawaii. And Governer Dole heard about it. He was so afraid they were going to raise up this revolutionary Hawaiian leader—The Big Five had already put down one revolution—and grab control of the islands. So Governor Dole's co-workers were afraid of this young revolutionary leader coming up, so the Governor grabbed him—and used the word 'adopted,' and took him into the Governor Dole family.

"So here's this kid who'd been trained in Hawaii Hoomanamana, being raised by the Governor of Hawaii. So when the other *kahunas* and chanters were being put in jail for practicing paganism, they didn't dare touch Governor Dole's kid. So he was allowed to practice openly, and therefore Daddy Bray became the most prominent or famous 'chanter,' or *kahuna*, in the Hawaiian Islands."

So the Hopi leaders passed the word around. I told Daddy Bray to come to Hotevilla Village in Hopiland and ask for David's house (David Monongye, now deceased, was a leader of the Pumpkin Clan). Sure enough, the next day, Daddy Bray did come in with his daughter and son-in-law. He stopped for gas at a little gas pump at the Northeast edge of Hotevilla and said, "Where is David Monongye's house?"

They said, pointing, "Oh, they're down there waiting for you, Daddy Bray." So that made him feel good that he was already well known, you see?

So he went in and told his story. Of course the Hopis were polite but they were also very suspicious of him, because they could see he had *power*. They didn't know if he was a two-heart or not. Those Hopis had to be cautious.

After the meeting with the Hotevilla elders, the translator and interpreter for Traditional and Religious Leaders of Hopi Nation, Thomas Banyacya of Kyakotsmovi Village, or "New Oraibi," took us to Oraibi to meet with John Lansa, Badger Clan Chief of Oraibi. Banyacya introduced Daddy and told John and his group what had already been said in Hotevilla. So when it came John's turn to respond, he went into more details than they could in Hotevilla. And that was very good.

I think it was the following day when Banyacya took us to Shungopavi Village. We arrived there just before lunch. So while we were having lunch, the *chakmungwi* (the village announcer or town crier) got up on the rooftop and sent out the call that this dignitary was going to meet with them in Andrew Heremeqraftewa's kiva (Andrew was a spokesman for the Hopi Independent Nation).

So after lunch, we went down the ladder for that kiva meeting. Thomas went down first, then Daddy Bray, then I went down. By the time I was going down, they were all laughing. I thought they were laughing at me, which doesn't bother me any.

But as I sat down, Thomas says, "They're laughing because one old man in the back of the kiva—when he saw Daddy Bray coming down the ladder into the kiva—that old man said, "What village is that man from? His face is familiar, but I just can't place him." So Banyacya explained that Daddy Bray was from a village in the middle of the Pacific Ocean, one-third of the way around the world. Then I felt not so foolish because I wasn't the only one who thought he looked like a Hopi.

So down in the kiva they compared migration stories (that's the histories), the present problems, the future prophecies. The stories dovetailed perfectly. Bray had certain details they didn't have; they had certain details he didn't have. But you put them together, and you get a much more complete picture, which is the way it works when you meet with traditional people and they remember their histories—their oral histories.

In the process, the Hopis checked out a few key words to see if they were the same in Hawaiian language, because each and every original traditional nation is *also* supposed to have a couple of words in the Hopi language, which strengthens the Hopi's belief, or teaching, that when their Maasau (the Great Spirit of This Land and Life) split people up into different nations, He gave them each their different languages. But He gave a few words of the language He entrusted to the Hopi to every one of those original nations, as one of the signs, or symbols, when they reunite in these last days, that they really did all start from the same place, near where Grand Canyon is today.

But they couldn't find any Hawaiian words that dovetailed with the Hopi words. That was a mystery to them, because every other traditional person they had compared original languages with did have some words similar to Hopi words and with similar meanings.

During that meeting at Shungopovy, they had told Daddy Bray from the Hopi knowledge how his people had reached the western shore of North America and *why* they had been sent from Heukovi Village in Hopiland to "go to the west as far as possible." Daddy didn't chant for them the Hawaiian history which tells where his twenty-four or twenty-seven generations of forefathers came from; he just told the Hopi elders verbally that he knew his forefathers came from the shores of Kahikiku, which the anthropology professors at that time said was Tahiti.

"But it means 'sunrise,'" he told them. "We came from North America. The place we set sail from on the coast of North America had gigantic trees growing right next to the ocean, which is what we made the dugout canoes out of to go to Hawaii. Due east of that shore of Kahikiku is a great grey mountain with snow on it all year round."

Well, there are three places on the coast of North America which fit that description, and all three places have stories of Indians that just disappeared overnight. The people who stayed behind don't know where they went, or where they came from. The strange people just mysteriously appeared, stayed around for awhile until they learned how to work with the ocean, and then suddenly disappeared.

So I don't know if it's down at Big Sur—those Esalen Indians—that his forefathers set sail from, or up at Humboldt Bay, west of Mt. Shasta, or the mainland off the northern tip of Vancouver Island in British Columbia, which is due west of Mt. Waddington, the highest mountain on the coast of North America (except Alaska). But we do know that they left the coast of North America, and to this day, after some of the Pacific storms, some of those great big logs from the Pacific Northwest wash ashore on the beaches of the Hawaiian Islands with the name "Weyerhauser" stamped on their butts. Weyerhauser is one of the biggest logging companies in Northwest America. So there are currents and winds that can take people to Hawaii, even if they're just riding a big log stamped with "Weyerhauser" on the butt.

When he finished with his Hawaiian history, the Hopi elders, through Banyacya, their Translator and Interpreter, told him about the Village of Heukovi (Sun Clan People) being given instructions by Maasau to go to the West as far as possible, because there were people out there that were in big trouble and needed help. Hopis knew those Sun People left Heukovi Village and finally reached the coast of California, but they didn't know anybody had enough courage and enough strength, were sincere enough in their religion and brave enough to keep on going to the west *after* they reached the Pacific Coast, 'til Daddy Bray came back to Hopiland with his report of dove-tailing traditional histories.

Now I've been with those California Shoshone Coastal Indians when they sing their Bird Dance Songs. Even the dancers usually don't know what those songs *really* are saying. People sing them to have a good time, dancing back and forth all night.

Those California Shoshones are descended from Hopi. It's verified in their language and their Bird Dance Songs. But that's what those Bird Dance Songs are: the heroes who led them on those migrations are given the names of birds, and the dance is the migration route from Hopiland: where they left the Grand Canyon area, to the Colorado River where they crossed it, what canyons they came up and what passes they came over, to reach Southern California. That's the way they remember their histories, as far as that migration is concerned.

Well, Daddy Bray checked through and it was either twenty-four or twenty-seven generations before (he knew but I've forgotten which figure it is) that his forefathers left the shores of Kahikiku, and so it's been maybe as much as a thousand years since Hopi had received any word from "the people who went to the west as far as possible." Daddy Bray's report was the first word the Hopi had gotten back again from those people. Yes, those oral traditions, those verbal histories, were still accurate enough so they were easily recognized and positively identified by all concerned. So words don't have to be written down in black and white to be remembered.

When they were all finished with their meeting there in the Shungopovi kiva, Daddy asked if he could leave a blessing for them before departing. The Hopi said they would appreciate that. So then he brought out his spiritual "gift," his voice, his chant. He sang his Hawaiian blessing chant, and I noticed some of the old men looking at each other out of the corner of their eyes down in that kiva. Some time later Thomas Banyacya asked me, "Did you see those two old men looking at each other out of the corners of their eyes down in the kiva? Do you know what that was about?"

I said, "No."

He said, "Well, that sacred chant, that Blessing Chant that Daddy Bray was singing for us was almost exactly one of the most sacred chants that's sung in the kiva. It's so sacred it's never even sung above ground. It's just sung in the kiva."

So when the Hopi heard that Blessing Chant in the kiva, then that clinched it. Because in that ancient chant, he was using the ancient Hawaiian language, and there were revealed the Hopi words that they were searching for.

Since then, I've been to Hawaii myself, and Craig Thurston of Clear Light Productions told me that from his studies the missionaries had somehow changed the Hawaiian language and taken all the "r's" out and replaced them with "l's." So that Haleakala Crater is really Hareakara—like Ra in Egypt, for the Home of The Sun.

Daddy Bray's *kahuna* ancestors were not descended from royalty. They were descended from the strongest *kahuna* in Hawaiian history, a man named Hewahewa. Those Sun Clan people of Hopi came over to Hawaii to straighten out those people who were practicing cannibalism, and blood rituals and ancestor worship as opposed to Creator worship. There were still "aloha spirit" pacifists there in Hawaii when Bray's ancestors arrived, but they were really being crushed in a hurry, and needed these powerful pacifist Hopis

39

to go in there and straighten out those bloody dictators. They weren't straightened out completely, but at least the pacifists survived to this day. The Peaceful People (that is what the word Hopi means) are still there, and the "aloha spirit" survives in Hawaii. So Daddy Bray's family are Sun Clan people and so he was named for the sun. His Hawaiian name means, in English, "The Seeing Eye of The Sun." Daddy Bray and Hopi Sun Clan Leader Dan Katchongva were, therefore, brothers.

Craig was just warming up, because no sooner did he finish this story than he launched into another one. I will include this story also, because it is a wondrous testimony to the magical power of chanting.

"I saw Daddy Bray chant a car up a hill one time," he said, settling into a new story about the time when he was in Hopiland with Daddy Bray and another co-worker, retired Brigadier Army General Herbert C. Holdridge. It was in late November of 1959, as he remembered, and the General was driving his light yellow Ford Victoria Coupe, a two-door sedan. There was a big snow storm raging as they drove toward Flagstaff, heading home to Los Angeles. They tried to get chains in Flagstaff, but there were none available.

Daddy Bray was sitting next to General in the front seat and I was sitting in the back seat. Well, we got to a point in the rapidly darkening afternoon, where I thought we were almost to the top of the rim descending into warmer and relatively snowless Oak Creek Canyon. But we had this hill to go up. There was first of all a little curve with the guard rail on the east side. The road went up a little hill, then flattened off, then went up another little hill. But we couldn't get up that first little hill because the road was too slippery. By then the highway was covered with snow, so you couldn't see the white line and you couldn't see where the black top left off and the dirt shoulder began. There was a car already parked in the middle of the road ahead of us; it couldn't get up that hill either. Two other cars were already in the ditch on the right hand side and they had their engines running to keep warm.

We tried to get up that hill two or three times and couldn't make it. Finally we were partway up the hill, stuck there. The General pulled on the emergency brake, and put the automatic transmission in "park." He kept the motor running so we could keep warm and he said to me, his 'native guide': "Now what do we do?"

I said, "Well, if somebody just pushes the car and you keep the tires spinning very slowly, it may bite on enough fresh snow so we can make it."

And Daddy Bray said, "You're not gonna make me push this car, are you?" I thought he was talking to me, but he wasn't. He said, "I'm an old man. I never been in this white stuff before. I understand it's slippery, and I might fall down and hurt myself. So it's not right to treat an old man that way." He was right, of course, and so I was really feeling guilty by that time.

So I said, "Another alternative is for all three of us to get out and start gathering firewood as quick as we can and as much as we can because it is getting dark *fast*—because I'm going to build two big fires and let you two old men sleep between the fires in those Army blankets you got on the back window, and I'm going to keep the fires going all night until we get some help here."

General asked, "How soon will the help come?"

I said, "I don't know. Sometimes these roads are snowed in for days out here. I don't know when the help is coming. It might be on the way here right now for all I know. But we'd better get ready for a long, cold and miserable night, because it's almost dark."

But before I could push the seat forward to get out of the car and start gathering firewood, Daddy Bray started chanting. Talk about the hair on the back of your neck standing up! Boy, it sure did! The General was sitting right in front of me and I watched him twitch and jerk as if he was going into convulsions, and I was *scared*. I thought, "What in the heck is going on here?" I didn't understand that language that Daddy Bray was chanting.

Suddenly, the car started to move uphill. The farther it went, the faster it went. When it got to going about twelve miles an hour, the General finally realized what was going on. He shifted *out* of "park" and took the emergency brake *off*, and started stepping on the accelerator. He was spinning the wheels but it didn't make any difference. We still kept going about twelve miles an hour. We kept right on going around that car that was parked in the middle of the road. The people in that car were looking at us with great big saucer eyes, you know. The guys on the side of the road that had slipped off in the ditch, they were looking at us with wide old eyes too, and we went right on up over that hill. After that, the road dipped down and there were snow flurries all the way to Phoenix, but it wasn't sticking to the road, so we were home free.

When I got to L.A., I found out that was the first snow in Phoenix in forty years. It wasn't enough to cover the road, but there was snow. It was really one tremendous storm. Before that storm ended, three elk hunters died of exposure out there on the Mogollon Rim, because they couldn't get back to the highway. So it was one big storm, and it was really a *great* test. I don't know what that car weighed—a ton-and-a-half, with three guys in it? But Daddy Bray just sat there and chanted and up the hill it went, in "park" and with the emergency brake pulled tight. Boy oh boy! What an experience!

I felt honored to hear this story first-hand. Craig Carpenter was trained to be an astute observer, so it isn't likely that this story was just a product of his imagination. I know several other people who met Daddy Bray and spoke of his powers with the greatest admiration—including one highly reputable lawyer.

In discussing this experience with Craig, he added:

I know what Gods Papa called upon to remove the obstacles in his path that snow-bound evening. I heard him call their official names or titles. They are in the lineage of the greatest Hawaiian Kahuna, Hewahewa.

All the Indian miracle-manifestors I knew and know, including Horn Chips (Victor Youngbear, the strongest of the thirteen Lakota miracle men), and Lame Deer (John Fire, most famous of the thirteen Miracle Men of the 1960s to 1970s) sang specific songs to invoke specific spirit persons, gods, to exercise or manifest their specific talents or miracle gifts. It seems to me to be that way with miracle manifestors in original cultures all over the world. We are spiritualists begging for help from spirit persons with higher powers, higher compassion or higher intelligence than we have. We are not "empowering" ourselves because "we are merely instruments of the Gods," as Daddy used to say so often.[9]

I wanted to share this story with you to inspire you with the thought that the human voice is a divine vehicle that connects us with Spirit. I believe that if we can allow Spirit to flow into and through us, our voices can literally carry us over the mountain tops!

5

SONGS OF OPPRESSION AND FREEDOM

Sing it out loud
Sing a song of freedom, brothers,
We gotta sing about it
We gotta shout out the joy!
            —Bob Marley

Why were the Hawaiian chanters thrown in jail?[1] Why were the Sun Dance, Yuwipi, and other Oglala and Lakota ceremonies outlawed from 1883 to 1963?[2] Why were black slaves forbidden to dance and play the fiddle?[3] The suppression of rituals, songs and dances has been lightly passed over in our history books—written off as if the government and missionaries were protecting these poor primitive savages from the obvious sins of idolatry.

For a country built upon the ideals of religious freedom, we have been astoundingly disrespectful of the spiritual practices of the people who treated us with hospitality and generosity when our ancestors arrived on their soil. In retrospect, we might ask: (1) How powerful are songs and rituals for making people feel good about themselves—in touch with their personal power and their sensuality? (2) How powerful are songs and rituals for unifying people, making them unwilling to tolerate oppression and thereby fomenting revolution?

Captain Cook arrived on the Hawaiian Islands in 1778. In those days, the *hula* was a sacred ceremony that combined poetry, music, pantomime and dance. The school was a temple and the dance teacher was the priest or priestess. Girls were taught to move their bodies in the sensual *hula* movements by swaying with the palm trees bending in the wind, and by undulating their hips in rhythm to ocean waves pounding on the shores. When they chanted about the rain, everyone knew they were also singing about making love. There was a joy and innocence that was incomprehensible to the westerners who arrived on their shores.

As the missionaries watched these beautiful unashamed young women with their uncovered breasts, dancing with the sensuous movements of the *hula,* they were seized by a fervor to rescue these "ignorant natives" from "the sins of idolatry." The *hula* and chanting were made illegal. By 1933, the Hawaiians who had once had complex chants and hulas for virtually every occasion, knew only a few of the most common chants and hulas.[4]

One of the first things that conquering priests and missionaries do with the children of subjugated people is to teach them to sing hymns. In the South, black slaves were not allowed to play the fiddle or to dance, but these ingenious people took the hymns of their oppressors and turned them into songs of hope and joy. The black preachers of those days would comfort and strengthen their people, reminding them, "You are created in God's image. You are not slaves, you are not 'niggers'; you are God's children."

The slaves figured they had one-up on their masters when judgment time came. Since the white folks had so much power, they could hardly resist the temptation to consider themselves above the law. The slaves knew they were having their hell now, so their masters would surely have theirs later. There was a hidden victory in songs like this:

> I got wings,
> You got wings,
> All God's children got wings.

In the Bible, the Prophet Jeremiah, overcome by events in his life and in Israel, asks, "Is there no balm in Gilead? Is no physician there?" The Negro Spiritual turns this into a song of triumph:

> There is a balm in Gilead,
> To make the spirit whole.
> There is a balm in Gilead,
> To heal the sin-sick soul.

In more recent times, the protest movements were full of "peace songs." Many of them, like "We Shall Overcome," were inspired by the old Negro Spirituals.[5]

Oppression was not limited to the United States. In the 1920s, many of the Jamaican blacks were in open rebellion against the British. Preacher Marcus Garvey was a pacifist who started a "Back to Africa" movement which became known as Rastafarianism.

The Rastafarians saw the Jamaican police and the Roman Catholic Church as agents of Babylon—a symbol of the oppression of the masses for the benefit of the privileged few. On the other hand, Zion was the promised land, the city of God, and Africa was the black Zion.

In the late 1960s, reggae music became the non-violent method of communicating the Rastafarians' message, as described by Virginia Lee Jacobs in her book, *The Roots of Rastafari*.

> Language among the Rastafarians is regarded as a "holy tool," and beyond the function of mere communication.... The Rastafarians understand the phenomenon of word, sound and power. Positive use of words creates positive energy and perhaps this is the whole basis of reggae music, which is used as a tool to uplift the world through "positive musical vibration."....
>
> The Rastafarians [also] believe in the word power of "chanting down" evil....
>
> [Bob Marley] believes that through positive musical vibration,

the children of Zion will be awakened to transcend the destruction of Babylon. Realizing that direct confrontation with Babylon will not work, Marley's political anger over the injustices dealt the black man at the hand of white imperialists is cleverly disguised in the chanted lyrics of his songs.

Most Reggae songs will express one or two basic thoughts, which are repeated over and over again like a mantra, to totally penetrate into the consciousness of the listener [who].... Marley reminds to "Get up, stand up for your rights." Jimmy Cliff advises, "Treat the youths right instead of giving them a fight, or it will be dynamite."

Reggae Singer Bob Marley and a few other popular Reggae musicians are referred to by some people as High Priests and Prophets, with ganja (marijuana) as their sacrament.

Indeed the whole experience of a reggae concert is like a spiritual revelation. The concert itself is like a ritualized Rastafarian mass, with the musicians acting as the high priests. Usually before the concert begins, there is a benediction to Jah Rastafari followed by a moment of silence. The captive audience is finally released from suspension by an onslaught of reggae rhythm which does not let up for hours.[6]

Yet another use of chanting and toning during times of oppression can be seen among the Tibetans. In 1959, China invaded Tibet, a tiny country in the Himalayan Mountains that was ruled by monks. The Chinese destroyed the ancient monasteries, and the monks who escaped went into exile. Today, the Dalai Lama heads his own government in north India.

The Gyume College of Tantric Buddhism is part of the Galugpa Sect (Yellow Hat), a form of tantric Buddhism founded by Tsongkapa (1357-1419). These monks have toured North America many times, demonstrating their extraordinary overtone chanting. During peaceful times, this remarkable chanting would be part of a ritual in which the monks would fast, and the chanting might continue for up to three days. The overtone chanting would not ordinarily be used outside of the sacred context, except during a time of national emergency. This time of forced exile from their homeland seems to constitute such an emergency; through these tours, they are attempting to communicate their culture and their political dilemma to the people of the world.

I have heard the Gyume monks, and their overtone chanting is full of uncanny deep sounds, together with high overtones, at times mixed with the loud clanging and booming of their most unusual gongs and drums, creating the hynotic effect of an orderly procession of lumbering elephants.

An overtone is the higher-pitched sound that you sometimes hear when a singer is making a single tone and another tone seems to jump off of it and echo from somewhere else. A singer with a resonant voice can create one overtone fairly easily, but the Gyume monks typically create two or more overtones, and the result is unworldly. In order to make these strange gutteral rumblings, the Tibetan monks change the position of the larynx to sound the lower-pitched fundamental of the OM, upon which they build the quality of the overtones.[7]

Dr. Bradford S. Weeks first heard Tibetan overtone chanting in North America in 1985, after which he went to their monastery in India. He explains that they practice the ancient *hooni* or throat singing, which enables a monk to chant three notes simultaneously, so that one monk can chant a three-note chord. Without mastery of the technique, Dr. Weeks says, "herniations, respiratory acid-base disturbances, esophageal lacerations and a variety of traumas to the throat have occurred."

"Speaking technically," says Dr. Weeks, "the goal for the monks is to make their bones sing, thus sparing their throats." Weeks refers to the unorthodox theories of Dr. Tomatis to explain how this is done.

> Dr. Alfred A. Tomatis, an authority in auditory neurophysiology, claims that hearing occurs primarily as a result of sound conduction through the bones of the head, and is not due to sound conduction through the ossicles of the ear. He feels the primary site for sound transmission and hearing is the portion of skull bones that runs from the tympanic sulcus (a groove in the skull bone at the point of attachment to the tympanic membrane) along the petrous bone of the skull.

In this article, Weeks quotes Dr. Tomatis's explanation of what occurs when the Tibetan monks chant: " 'As the bow sets violin strings vibrating, but it is the violin body which sings, so with proper chanting posture, the larynx of the monks contacts the vertebral column thereby setting the axial bones to singing' (Tomatis, 1986)."[8]

As we listen to these unusual sounds, perhaps our own axial bones fall into a sympathetic vibration with theirs, which stimulates the pineal and pituitary glands. This may explain why this chanting has the peculiar ability to put some of us into a deep trance. The sound is intended to create the feeling—especially for the chanters themselves—of being like the gods.

Their chanting reminds me of the Kachinas I saw at Hopiland, regaled in incredible masks and costumes, representing the gods coming down from the mountains. As I recall, a group of about twenty men stayed in the kiva, fasting for three days and then they emerged in full costume, dancing in a slow, majestic procession around the plaza, chanting a continual deep hypnotic chant in rhythm to the bells on their ankles and the rattles in their hands.

The Hopi were one of the only tribes in this country who steadfastly refused to give up their own spiritual teachings, and consequently their ceremonial dances have continued without disruption until the present time. The elders absolutely refused to send their children to boarding school, and *all of the leading men* were put in jail for an entire winter. Still, many of the people persisted in keeping their children at home and jailings continued for years, with some of the men put into maximum security at Alcatraz Island. Some Hopi finally relented, but others "remained faithful" and to this day have kept the children out of even the local dayschool.

Indian children throughout the United States were forced to go to these schools where they were separated from their parents and their communities, not allowed to speak their own languages, forbidden to practice their own rituals and taught to be ashamed of their own cultures.

Many tribes apparently surrendered to the pressures of the government and missionaries, assimilating the new religions. Still, there were small groups of Traditionalists who continued to practice the old ways as often as they could, despite the teasing and derision they received at the hands of their western-educated youth.[9]

In the sixties, the disillusioned children of the dominant culture became desperate for more meaning in their lives, and they starting swarming onto the reservations, looking for elders to teach them how to live close to the land. The Indian youths who had been taught to be ashamed of their elders were shocked by this peculiar turn of events, and it was one of many factors that led to a reawakening of traditional American Indian teachings and a revival of interest in the old ceremonies.

Ed McGaa, also known as Eagle Man, is an American Indian lawyer who was raised at the Lakota reservation in South Dakota. Like the other kids, he was sent off to the missionary boarding school, but when his sister died of pneumonia, his mother found excuses to keep him at home. His grandmother taught him the old ways, and two holy men, Fools Crow and Eagle Feather, were his mentors.

In *Mother Earth Spirituality*, he tells about how he left the traditional path and then returned to it again as a teenager, when he saw the Sun Dance for the first time.

> Bill Eagle Feather, the Rosebud holy man, boldly defied the missionaries and brought our sacred Sun Dance out into the open. I watched as Fools Crow, the Oglala holy man, pierced Bill, the lone sun dancer.... I can still recall Bill standing alone beneath the Sun Dance tree and pulling backward, his taut skin stretched, pulling upon his rawhide braided rope.

After that incident, the young people started coming back to the old ways. McGaa went to Vietnam, and before he left, he had a special stone blessed for him, in a ritual intended to protect him in battle. He pledged that if he returned safely, he would participate in the Sun Dance. After flying numerous missions, he returned victorious to his reservation, only to find it being taken over by the missionary.

> I watched the missionary drive his pickup into the arena and stop the dance so that he could celebrate Mass at the base of the Sun Dance tree. Although he held Mass in the church fifty-two weeks of the year, on this occasion he felt that he had to impose his ceremony over ours. His portable altar was unloaded, and I had to watch a non-Indian ceremony take precedence over our people's ceremony right on my own reservation.
>
> ...The tribal council, stacked with his church members, had decreed that the Sun Dance would last only three days, Thursday, Friday, and Saturday. Saturday would be the piercing day [instead of Sunday, as it was usually done]. On Sunday, the missionary would say his Mass at the base of the Sun Dance tree.
>
> ...The dancers and holy men were too afraid to challenge the authority of both the priest and the tribal council. All pierced on the third day. I did not. I had been in the Marines and had flown combat in Vietnam. My warrior's blood was up, and I was not afraid of the missionary. He shook his fist at me and told me that I must put his God into our ceremony. When I would not relent, he claimed to have some special knowledge or power to predict that my spirit would not go to a good place. I felt that he was making preposterous statements and told him so. He alluded again to his special powers and suggested that I was possessed by the devil. I was glad that I was a traditional Sioux; since we do not have a concept of the devil, he was not able to use that age-old tactic to scare me into submission.

...On the fourth day, I was the lone sun dancer. Fools Crow pierced me, and an old man named Loon stood beside me with a cane. He was half-blind and half-crippled, but he threatened to hit anybody who attempted to stop the piercing. I had challenged a lot of authority and caused a great deal of commotion, but the Sun Dance that year went the full four days.

The following year, when the priest tried to disrupt the ceremony, the young people of the tribe surrounded him and made it clear that he wasn't welcome. Since then, young people have taken part in increasing numbers.[10]

From the examples in this chapter, we have seen how song has been used to protest political oppression. Now let us look at something that is even more subtle: sexual oppression.

6

REJOINING BODY AND SONG

The sense of guilt and shame that we in Judeo-Christian cultures are encouraged to feel about our sexuality, and the censorship and control of song, dance and rituals that we have seen, are in sharp contrast to nature-based societies in which sexuality, song and dance are enjoyed and encouraged. Song seems to be the key to unraveling the mystery; through understanding how song and dance have been controlled and censored, we eventually come face-to-face with our own unspoken and unconscious taboos.

Cultures that are natural, that flow with the seasons of nature, that honor places in nature as sacred; that honor women and their sexual and reproductive rights—i.e., hunting, gathering and home industry societies where people generally provide or trade for their own food and resources—are a threat to the inherently unnatural society that we live in, a society that exploits women and men, exploits sexuality and exploits nature—i.e., agricultural-industrial societies that divide up and own land and natural resources, and require cheap labor and consumers.

Knowing this helps us to understand why cultures that are nature-oriented are said to be worshipping idols (defined as "false gods" since they are not the official god) and why natural expressions of the body including song, dance, sexuality and reproduction have—at various times and in various situations—been controlled, censored, repressed and made a source of shame and embarrassment.

This shame and embarrassment about sexuality, and the connection with dancing, is seen in this statement by Kathleen, the woman who spoke in tongues when she was a teenager with the Pentecostal Church. Since she obviously enjoyed the experience of "being seized by the Holy Spirit," I asked her why she left the church. This was her reply:

> It was hard enough, just being a teenager. Our church wouldn't allow dancing. No dancing. No make-up. Only whores and wild women did things like that.[1]

To understand this association of singing and dancing with "whores and wild women," we need to go back to ancient times. Evidence is strong that our current patriarchal society was preceeded by ancient matrilineal times (matrilineal refers to lineage being passed through the mother—as distinct from matriarchal, which refers to rulership by women) when women and children were not considered the property of men, and sexuality took many forms. Partnerships between men and women came and went, while the children always had a stable home with their mothers and grandmothers. Their uncles (the mother's brothers) provided stable male figures in their lives.

Children were cared for by the whole community, and particularly by a large group of kin, who all lived nearby. Since inheritance was not passed through the paternal line, it was not essential to know who the child's blood father was. It was only after the institution of the patriarchy that virginity at marriage and concepts like chastity, purity and modesty became popular.[2]

The matrilineal mode of organization was consistent with the Mother Goddess religion and the fertility rites that were a part of all ancient civilizations, under the names of Isis, Aphrodite, Venus, Parvati, Ceres, Mylitta and others. Temple priestesses were trained in the art of using their vital life force energy ("shakti" as it is called by the Hindus) in combination with their spiritual energy. These women were well versed in the arts of song and dance, which were combined with their shakti, in various rituals designed to honor the goddess and promote fertility for the people and for the crops.[3]

The Australian Aborigines believe that their own erotic experiences have an effect upon surrounding life processes, and that the sexual energies of human beings and nature have an effect upon each other.

> The view that both humans and nature rely on metaphysical erotic sources persisted in all early societies before the crackdown on fertility rites by state religions, especially Christianity and Islam. In the dreadful course of events in Europe between the eleventh and sixteenth centuries, inquisitions and witch hunts destroyed the rites of exchanging sexual and erotic vitality between humans and nature.[4]

In matrilineal times, sexuality was celebrated. On certain festival days, it was considered appropriate to find pleasure with partners other than the usual ones. The Australian Aborigines still have festival days in which open sexual expression is encouraged,[5] and many indigenous people had similar celebrations before the arrival of the missionaries.

In south India in the ninth and tenth centuries, magnificent temples were built, adorned with *devadasis*, handmaidens of the gods. According to legend, the gods were accustomed to having *apsaras*, celestial nymphs, sing and dance for them. It was considered good luck for a family to dedicate their daughters to the temple of Surya, and great good fortune for the young women. The ruins of these temples can still be seen, with sensual female figures dancing, playing drums, and openly, joyfully copulating or otherwise engaged with male figures and with each other.

At some point, the situation began to change and temple priestesses became temple prostitutes. Nevertheless, it was not too bad a life for these women. In Tanjore, King Rajaraja had four hundred *devadasis* installed in his temple. Families would present their daughters to be married to the deity of the temple. Since they were married to the god, they could never become widows, and would always be taken care of. Like the geishas of Japan, these women were well educated, skilled in song, dance and languages. They were highly respected in India, and their divine presence at weddings, births and formal public functions such as ships' arrivals and feasts was considered propitious. They were often quite wealthy, having been generously gifted with extravagant jewels and vast lands.

During Muslim rule in north India, they were called *tavaifs*, and the sons of the upper classes were sent to them to round off their education. This tradition continued into modern times, and even in the early part of this century, some highly respected British, Muslim and Indian men mingled openly with *tavaifs*.

In south India, the rights of the *devadasis* were recognized as they were in British India. Their way of life was based on matrilineal law, with property being passed from mother to daughter. The daughters followed their mother's profession and the sons became musicians and dance teachers. These families set a standard for the practice and theory of dance and music, and some of the highly accomplished musicians of modern India are descended from these family lines.

An unfortunate side-effect was that ordinary women were discouraged from singing and dancing, since "only the *devadasis* needed these arts." Hence, the idea that dancing be reserved for "whores and wild women."

After the turn of the century, with increasing western influence, the *devadasis* came to be seen as something to be exploited, and the Brahmin priests made a fat profit from them. The temples lost their spiritual fervor and the western-educated Indians were distressed by any association between sexuality and spirituality. The women of the temples were no longer well educated, and the artists associated with the temples were neglected. When the victorian missionary ladies arrived in south India, they were "absolutely shocked and appalled" by the open activities of these women. They put pressure on the British administrators and the Indian princes, and the dedication of *devadasis* was stopped by 1930.[6]

In various ancient cultures, the vagina and penis—the *yoni* and *lingam* to the Hindus—were considered sacred and honored as symbols of fertility. India is resplendent with sacred rocks that have these unmistakable shapes.[7] In Hawaii, there is a cave that is sacred to the goddess, in the distinct shape of a *yoni*. Artwork and sacred objects of virtually every culture are rich with full-bosomed women and yawning yonis.

The Australian Aborigines consider the mouth to be the male equivalent of the vagina. The vagina gives birth to things of the earth. With proper training, an Aborigine male can enter the Dreamtime and use his mouth to give birth to certain sounds that can change reality *before* it occurs.[8]

The *yoni* and the mouth are our two most powerful sources of creativity. Since women have both yonis and mouths, they have a distinct advantage. When one person has more power than another, there are two ways of dealing with the situation. Our Judeo-Christian ancestry goes back, in biblical legend, to Esau and Jacob, the twin sons of Isaac. Esau was born first, so he was considered the elder, and entitled to the main blessing of his father. When Isaac was old and blind and close to death, he asked to have Esau brought to him. Instead, Jacob was wrapped in furs and disguised as his hairy brother, thereby stealing his father's blessing by deception. This is one way to deal with a difficult situation. It is the American way. Ask any Indian.

Western cultures have responded to this inequality of creative power by stealing the birthright away from women. Then, to cover up their guilt, they point their fingers at the women. We see this in the biblical legend of Adam and Eve. The serpent is the kundalini power—the essential sexual creative energy. Eve is aligned with the serpent, and "tempts" Adam to eat of the apple. Pity poor Adam and Eve whose angry god raged against them and shamed them, thereby condemning them to a Hell of their own making.

The conventional Judeo-Christian fear of sexual energy is reflected in a deep distrust of the feminine: dancing, sexuality, psychic energy, trance states and mind-altering plants. All of these things have, at various times, been said to be "of the devil," "evil," and finally, illegal.

Growing up in this society generally means that as children, most of us are taught to squelch our emotions, to stay calm, and be quiet. We are taught to be ashamed of our sexual energy and of our genitals. No wonder we grow up feeling as if the passion we secretly long to express is forbidden.

There is an intimate connection between the mouth and the genitals. Midwives know that when a woman is tight down below, if she opens her mouth wide, her vagina will instantly relax.

Just because we grew up in a tradition of repression doesn't mean we have to perpetuate it. There are other ways to be, and other ways to raise our children. We might take inspiration from the Australian Aborigines.

In Robert Lawlor's delightful book, *Voices of the First Day*, he says that "Gutsy, raunchy, vivacious spirits of nature, known as the Mimi Spirits, taught sexuality to the Aborigines in all its diverse forms." The women are knowledgeable about herbal birth control and abortion. They space their children as they want them, so there is no problem with overpopulation, and there are no unwanted children, no juvenile delinquents, and no rape or sexual violence. Their children—whom anthropologists describe as extraordinarily happy—are raised to have a joyful relationship with their bodies and their sexuality. They grow up to be unusually healthy adults who are well adjusted psychologically and sexually, and highly evolved spiritually.

The Aborigines believe that it is the role of women to act on the physical plane, on the earth.

> Her primary function is maintaining harmonious relationships between human and psychic energies within society, as well as the harmony of human society with the earth. Women are the hidden force behind the sacred attitudes that allow the earth to remain a generative field that nourishes and sustains life.

The men, on the other hand, are hunters who must deal with death on a daily basis. It is their work to enter the Dreamtime and maintain balance in that sphere *before* it becomes materialized. For over 100,000 years, Australian Aborigine men have been developing an alternate source of creative power.

Immediately after the circumcision rite, the young man is presented with two bullroarers and told that these are his new parents, and he should call on them to meet his needs. The bullroarers hold the hypnotic power that gives him entry into the Dreamtime. He has learned to enter this realm through a ritual that involves a blood sacrifice of a part of his own reproductive organ. While he was recovering from this ordeal, the old men began to initiate him into the sacred use of certain sounds that would eventually enable him to become an active participant in the creative unfolding of the universe.

This is not the easy way to participate in creativity. Learning to enter and interact with the Dreamtime requires profound dedication, discipline, and self-sacrifice. Most young boys are not willing to make such a sacrifice, and that is why they have to be "seized" or "grabbed" by the older men and psychically whipped into submission until they enter into a trance. But once the boy gets a taste of it, he is hooked. The experience of ecstasy that goes with the trance state is the reward for doing it.

Before hunting, the men do rituals to increase the potency of the species they intend to hunt.

> Men...learn the vibrational rhythms and specific "seed sounds" that coagulate (increase) or disperse (decrease) the premanifesting energies of that species....in Aboriginal cosmology, the earth's mag-

netism or Rainbow Serpent created the creatures of this world by pronouncing the name of the seed sound of that species at the place where the potency of that creature was deposited in the Dreamtime.[8]

Seed sounds are tones which include vowel sounds that have powerful properties to increase and decrease energies before they manifest on the material plane. These are tones that have been used in ancient cultures throughout the world.

Perhaps in this concept of seed sounds we can find the key for rejoining body and song. The seed of the body is in the genitals. Human increase and decrease depends upon the fertility or sterility of our seeds. Might there be sounds which influence the increase and decrease of all of life—and specific sounds that influence specific forms of life?

Could it be that when all our chakras are open and vibrating, when we are in full possession of our sexual, emotional and spiritual potency, people all over the planet will use these seed sounds like the OM of the Harmonic Convergence, to create transformation on a planetary level?

In the ancient language of Sanskrit, each spoken syllable is said to possess a vibratory power. This is also true of the ancient Tibetan language, of ancient sacred American Indian languages, and of the Hebrew language. In the religions of all these cultures, and others, prayers are chanted aloud, and their repetitive chanting has a hypnotic power upon those who chant and those who listen.

Charles Muir, teacher of Tantric Yoga, uses the Tibetan seed sounds that correspond to the chakras in the following way:

(1) Inhale and cover ears with thumbs, eyelids with index fingers, nose with third fingers, mouth with fourth and fifth fingers. Hold the breath for a minute and then exhale and release nose partially and make a sound like bees around the hive. Repeat several times.

(2) Inhale and cover the orifices, as described above, then exhale and chant all of these tones on one breath (do not say the numbers of the chakras aloud):

first chakra:	LAM
second chakra:	VAM
third chakra:	RAM
fourth chakra:	YAM
fifth chakra:	HAM
sixth chakra:	OM [9]

The sound for the crown chakra is "All Sound," or Soundless Sound. Like white light, it is the presence of all sound frequencies.

The Rosicrucians use the ancient Egyptian seed sounds for "spiritual preparation for conscious attunement," according to First Imperator Dr. H. Spencer Lewis. Each sound is full, resonant, and prolonged to the full extent of the breath. The first two sounds are done on a relatively low note (such as middle C); the second two sounds are done on a relatively high note (such as high C); and the last two sounds are done on the low note again (middle C).

> AUM
> AUM
>
> RAH
> MA
>
> AUM
> AUM [10]

The spontaneous emergence of interest in toning is like the phoenix arising out of the ashes of our crumbling civilization. It is like the first cries of an infant, full of potential to express raw emotions. Through toning, we may be able to connect with our true essence, our spirit, and with the Great Mystery.

But it is just the first step. Eventually we may feel the need to go into the wilderness, to find a mountain peak and cry for a vision. We may be drawn together in groups to blend our visions. Knowing that our energies and thoughts influence our reality, we may be inspired to ask for Guidance about how to bring about the miracles that will save the planet, and save those few remaining "wet and wild places" where the most powerful spirits dwell.

If there is to be a true healing of energies on this planet, we will have to find ways to honor and protect the lands and cultures of our most severely endangered species: the traditional spiritual leaders of the Hopi, the Australian Aborigines, the Hawaiian *kahunas*, and others. These are our ancestors—our kin—the elders of the human race. In the past two generations, our link with their ancient traditions has been almost completely broken. Today there are just a few faithful Traditionalists who are waiting, with very little hope, for us to return and mend that missing link.

7

WHAT IS TONING AND HOW DO YOU DO IT?

How many of us become great singers when left to the privacy of the shower? Or driving down the highway? Our ability to sing—especially spontaneously—relates directly to whether we feel free to express our emotions. When I was alone and in my private fantasy world, my voice could do things it could never do when I felt self-conscious, observed by others.

Like most people in western societies, I grew up learning to censor my emotions, my words, and every sound that came out of my mouth. I learned to make only sounds that were socially acceptable. As a child, I was taught not to make loud noises of any kind: boisterous laughter, painful crying, screaming with pleasure. Most adults, repressed as children, have a fear of the direct, emotional, gut-level expression of feelings.

I grew up feeling secretive and shy about using my voice in a forceful and passionate way. I harbored a secret desire to sing, yet singing felt mysteriously threatening. But when I was alone, it was different. I see myself at eight years old, in my mother's silk fuchsia robe, promenading down the long hallway of our Chicago home, past the elegant Chinese vases, making grand gestures while singing gut-wrenching arias in some foreign tongue. At that moment I half-expected to hear a knocking at the front door of a man in a top hat and waist-coat, who would doff his hat and bow to me. He would explain that he was a talent scout wandering through the neighborhood who had been lured to this house by the thrilling crescendoes of a female voice which sent chills up and down his spine. "Could that voice belong to you?" he would inquire.

I would nod demurely. He would kiss my hand, pressing it to his heart. "You, my dear, are the discovery of a lifetime."

Yet when I auditioned for the school chorus, I barely got in. I even took two or three singing lessons, but my teacher was not terribly impressed. My main vocal achievements for the next twenty years consisted of improvised lullabies to my babies and then, later, singing songs like "I'll Be Working on the Railroad" during long trips in the car with my boys.

I didn't get over my fear of singing until I started toning. It's not necessary to have a beautiful or a powerful voice to tone, and it's not possible to make mistakes!

I was living in Victoria, British Columbia, and teaching about "Color and Crystals" when I attended a workshop on "Toning for the Chakras," with singer and musician, Celeste Crowley. Her workshop helped me to break through my resistance to opening up my voice. Soon after, I incorporated the use of toning in my own workshops and began teaching about "Color, Sound and Crystals."

I still felt shy about *sounding* (another word for toning) in public, but I would tone with my students as we went through the chakras, a whole roomful of people toning together. Sometimes the room would reverberate with overtones bouncing off the ceiling—as if there were a chorus of angels on the rooftop.

Gradually I overcame my shyness. The feedback I received about my toning was so positive that it gave me confidence. The sounding took on a life of its own. It seemed to have its own intelligence and I learned to trust it. During meditations or talks or healings I would find myself overcome by the desire to make sounds. I just had to open my mouth and the sounds would come pouring out of me.

What is toning? Toning is utilizing the vibratory power of the voice by making long, sustained sounds, without the use of melody, beat or rhythm. We make these sounds by using a vowel, a consonant, or a combination of both, without the use of words or specific meaning. When we make these sounds, they cause vibrations which may create overtones that reverberate in a way that is incredibly penetrating.

Overtones are high sounds that emanate from a single musical note. These tones have a high frequency (number of vibrations per second in each soundwave). Many of the overtones are higher than our ear's ability to hear. This is called subliminal sound, and may explain why toning has the mysterious ability to put people into a trance-like state, or to invoke profound emotions. This book will not attempt to teach you how to make overtones deliberately, but overtones do tend to occur when you tone.

A tone may be high-pitched and piercing or it may be low-pitched and soothing—or anything in between. Any specific tone will have a fairly predictable effect on the person listening to it. High, piercing tones tend to speed up the heart, and low, soothing tones tend to slow it down. Harsh tones tend to cause a feeling of anxiety, and rich, mellow tones bring about a sense of deep inner peace. Some tones stir up strong feelings, and others pull us out of our emotions, into a meditative state.

Pleasant, low-pitched tones tend to produce a grounded, earthy, practical sense of well-being. Low tones are good for getting into your body and getting things accomplished. Pleasing, high-pitched tones can help you to release stress and transcend your day-to-day worries. They tend to produce a euphoric, angelic, other-worldly or deeply relaxed feeling. *It is not necessary to have a good singing voice to become proficient at toning.*

Understanding Musical Notation. Most of the exercises in this book do not require any musical knowledge. However, a few exercises are difficult to describe without using musical notes as a frame of reference. *It is not necessary to know how to read music to become proficient at toning.* Very few exercises in this book refer to musical notation. For the ones that do, the following explanation will make it possible for you to follow the instructions in this book *without* reading notes and without using a musical instrument.

Tones	Notes	Notation
DO	c (high)	
TI	b	
LA	a	
SO	g	
FA	f	
MI	e	
RE	d	
DO	c (middle)	

The chart should be read from the bottom, going up. Most of us are familiar with the use of the syllables, Do-Re-Mi-Fa-So-La-Ti-Do, and have heard these repeated in sequence, with the bottom "Do" being the lowest, deepest tone, and the top "Do" being the highest, with all the syllables in between going step-by-step from low to high.

A scale consists of a series of ascending and descending notes. Every scale in the standard diatonic system that is used in the west—except c major—has sharps and flats. If you look at a piano, it is a combination of white keys and black keyes. All of the "natural" notes are played on the white keys; the black keys are the sharps and flats. The scale of c major has no sharps or flats and that is the scale I've used above, under "notes."

An octave consists of eight notes, and all western scales have eight ascending and descending notes. Each note is on a different pitch, and each one of the eight notes of each octave has a letter designation: a, b, c, d, e, f, g, a. In this case there is a "low a" and "high a." The scale of c will begin with c, with seven notes going up from it, ending with another c at the eighth note: c, d, e, f, g, a, b, c. The scale of d will begin and end with d. The octaves that are most commonly used by the human voice and by most instruments are the two middle ones, on the piano. The note at the very center of the piano is called "middle c," and everything to the right of it, or "above" it will make progressively higher notes. Everything to the left of middle c or "below" it will make progressively lower notes. "High c" refers to the c one octave above middle c. "Low c" refers to the c one octave below middle c.

It doesn't matter whether you actually begin with the note c or some other note, as long as each sound is higher than the previous sound. Don't take it too seriously, or you might get intimidated. The important thing is to have a good time.

Each tone is a sustained sound (a vowel or consonant or syllable) made on a particular pitch (a musical note). For example, you can tone the sound EE on the pitch of b, or you can use the same sound on d. Or you can use other sounds such as OO or OM on the pitch of b, or on any other pitch.

Toning, chanting or droning are all similar practices that virtually all cultures have used, particularly in their religious services. Whether you grew up chanting AMEN, OM, or AMEIN in your church, mosque, or synagogue, or whether your army, tribe or football team made hollers or whoops, you have in all these ways experienced some form of toning.

Breathing. When you breathe fully, your heart slows and you feel calm and peaceful. The breath is the single most vital tool for attaining a sense of peace and calm, helping to eliminate the effects of stress. Most of the symptoms of aging are related to a deficiency of oxygen at the cellular level. Oxygen is essential for the health of the blood, skin, brain and every cell of the body. As we grow older, we use oxygen less efficiently. The consequent lack of oxygen that we experience as we age accounts for many of the symptoms that we associate with aging, including senility, which is caused— at least in part—by a deficiency of oxygen to the brain. Those who breathe deeply are bringing more oxygen into their blood.

Deep breathing is an essential part of meditation. This may be one reason why yogis and people who meditate regularly appear to be youthful and healthy even when they are very old.

Toning expands the abdomen and the lower lungs, pushing stale air out of the lungs, enabling us to absorb more fresh oxygenated air. You don't need to have strong breath control to begin toning, but the more toning you do, the greater your lung capacity will become. Since toning requires deep breathing, it contributes to health and a sense of peacefulness, helping to eliminate the effects of stress, and helping to prevent (and sometimes to heal) heart disease, asthma, bronchitis and senility.

Are you a shallow breather? If you're not sure, sit or stand in front of a mirror and observe yourself. Take off your shirt or wear a close-fitting top. When you inhale, can you see your chest or your abdomen expand? If your breath is deep, you will see it easily. But if, like most people, your breath is shallow, you will have to watch very carefully to see yourself breathing.

Shallow breathing contributes to a lack of oxygen in the body. The habit of shallow breathing begins in early childhood, when children are forced to be quiet, to be still, to hold back their feelings. When you're scared, you literally "hold your breath." You don't let a single sound escape, not even a sigh. When you're afraid of feeling angry, excited or sad, you don't like to breathe in, because a deep breath expands the heart or the abdomen, and the heart and abdomen are where you hide those intense emotions. (That's why children so often complain of "tummy aches" when they're emotionally upset.)

If you've been punished or judged for having these feelings ("Little boys don't cry." "Don't be a scaredy-cat." "Children are meant to be seen and not heard." "Big girls don't cry."), you may prefer not to take deep breaths and not to feel these feelings.

Women rarely breathe from their abdomens, because they believe that they look better with flat, rigid stomachs instead of relaxed, rounded ones. Women (and men) with rigid stomachs often have trouble with indigestion and may have trouble getting in touch with their feelings. You can't take full, deep abdominal breaths with a rigid stomach. Ultimately, the trick is to relax and remember to breathe from your abdomen.

The diaphragm is a muscular membrane that is located just below the lungs (see illus., p. 65). The stomach (upper abdomen) is just below the diaphragm. Abdominal breathing pulls the diaphragm down and expands the lower portion of the lungs. As you inhale, place your fingertips lightly at your stomach and feel this area rising with your breath. Practice until you are definitely breathing from your upper abdomen. Below the stomach and the navel are the intestines, or the lower abdomen. Inhale and place your fingertips lightly at your lower abdomen and feel this area rising with your breath. After practicing for awhile, abdominal breathing will begin to come naturally and you won't have to think about it. You will find yourself taking deep abdominal breaths throughout the day, and this alone will contribute to your health.

Here's an exercise to strengthen your diaphragm and give you better breath control.

Stand up, with your feet shoulder length apart (see illus., p. 66).

(1) Take a deep breath and feel your lower abdomen (below your navel) and then your upper abdomen (above your navel) expand, like a balloon. Your shoulders will rise slightly. Hold your

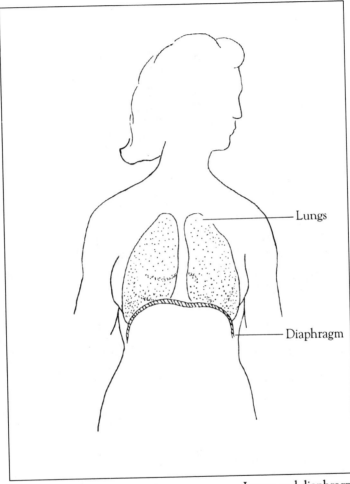

Lungs and diaphragm

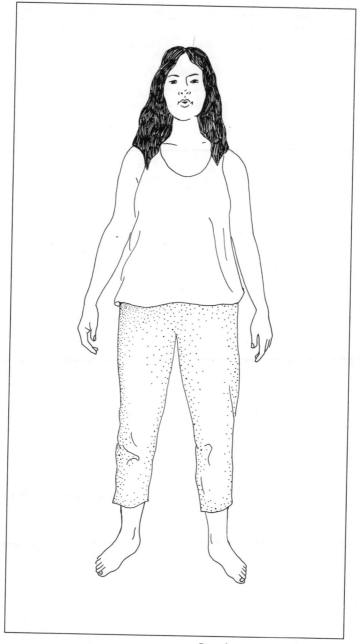

Standing position for toning

breath to the count of five and then—without exhaling—suck in your entire abdomen. Then push it out again. Then exhale and relax your entire abdomen. Practice until you can do this easily.

(2) Inhale as before and hold your breath. Suck in your abdomen and push it out as you did before, and then do it again. Exhale and relax your stomach. Continue practicing until you can suck in and push out your abdomen ten times while holding your breath.

How To Tone. When you're ready to tone, begin by inhaling through your nose. (Feel your lower and then upper abdomen expanding. Before they are fully expanded, feel your breath continue up into your lower and then upper lungs as they, too, expand as your shoulders rise slightly.) Release your breath through your mouth while making one long sustained sound. This is the tone. The sound will continue as long as you exhale. When you run out of breath, inhale again through your nose and exhale through your mouth, again making a long sustained sound. This procedure can be repeated as often as you like.

The best way to hold your body while toning is in a position that frees your diaphragm and abdomen (see illus., p. 68). For this reason, most singers stand when they sing. An alternate position, particularly when toning accompanies meditation, is to sit on your lower legs.

You can sit in a cross-legged position on the floor or you can sit on a chair, but be sure your spine is straight and your diaphragm and abdomen are unobstructed. If you're standing, imagine that the sound is coming up from your feet. If your body is inclined to sway as you stand or sit, just allow these natural rhythms to move through your body. Relax your jaw. When you make a sound, let your jaw hang open. It's good if your jaw is so relaxed that you can put your middle three fingers between your teeth, so your ring finger is touching your bottom teeth and your index finger is touching your top teeth.

When toning is used during a healing session, the person receiving the treatment may be lying down. This person may wish to participate in the toning. It's difficult, but perfectly all right to tone while lying down, or the person may want to stand or sit while toning and then lie down again.

Making Sounds. When toning, it's impossible to make a mistake. Vowels lend themselves well to toning. Here are some exercises that you can experiment with. If you do not have a tuning fork or a musical instrument, follow the procedure outlined above under the heading "Understanding Musical Notation."

Sitting positions for toning

—Tone a vowel on the note of your choice for as long as your breath allows. Repeat several times. (Example: Tone A as in "bay" on the note of d.)

—Tone the same sound on a different note. (Example: Tone A as in "bay" on the note of f.)

—Tone the same vowel on different octaves. (Example: Tone O as in "home" on middle c and then on high c.) Vary your sounds by doing the long version of the vowel and the short. (Example: O as in "home" and O as in "long" on middle c and then on high c.)

—Tone a syllable (a single uninterrupted sound formed by a vowel and one or more consonants) on the same note. Repeat several times. (Example: Tone OM on middle c.)

—Tone the same syllable on a different note, and repeat. (Example: Tone OM on the note of d.)

—Tone HA-HEY-HE-HO-HU, sounding each syllable on a different non-consecutive note. (Example: Tone HA on high c, HEY on low b, HE on middle d, HO on high a, and HU on high b.)

—Find a syllable and note combination that pleases you and tone it again and again. (Example: LA on a.)

Now let go entirely and play like a kid. Beat on the table top, hit a cup with a spoon, bang pots and pans together. Get silly. Loosen up. Make up a song in a pretend language that sounds Indian, Chinese or Greek.

You might get a drum with a natural skin that gives off lots of reverberations. Hit the drum repeatedly and try to imitate or blend your tones with its sounds. Do the same with a gong, bell, Tibetan bowl, or tuning fork. Do anything to experiment with sound and with the freeing of your voice.

If you feel inhibited about making sounds, don't worry, you're not alone. One way to overcome this resistance is to start by humming. Follow the exercises and hum instead of toning. When you get comfortable with humming, make a louder hum. As you notice that nothing terrible happens to you, you'll be able to make louder noises.

Here's another technique that a woman shared with me. She was driving alone in her car and suddenly she had a strong urge to tone. She had never done anything like that before, and she felt inhibited. As she told me this story, she shook her head and marvelled, "Do you understand? I was *all alone*, and yet I felt *embarrassed* to make a sound!"

She reassured herself, saying, "It's okay. Go ahead and squawk!" So she squawked for awhile. This helped her to overcome her worst fear: she could open her mouth and squawk—and nothing terrible happened. The squawking sounded ridiculous, but it didn't do any harm.

After squawking for awhile, she realized that she couldn't do anything worse, so it became easier to make other sounds. Experimenting with her voice, she found she could do all sorts of entertaining, amusing and scary things. Within months, without any instruction, she was making full, resonant, and pleasing sounds.

Overtones occur naturally when toning, especially when a whole group is toning together on the same pitch. There is an art and science of overtone chanting, as it is practiced by the Mongolians and the Tibetan Monks. A person can be trained to do this. But even without training, the overtones will come spontaneously, especially when you are feeling centered. Bradford Weeks, M.D., writes in Don Campbell's anthology, *Music Physician for Times to Come*:

> When I asked a Tibetan abbot about the technique of producing what some have called the "transcendent overtone" in his chanting, he said that there was no such thing, only an indefinable quality which may become audible when the degree of the monks' devotion is appropriate.[1]

The mouth is a natural resonator, and by slight adjustments of your jaw, cheeks, tongue and lips, you have the ability to make a great range of pitches. This is how we create language. The mouth and its adjacent vocal cavities are capable of making two different pitches at the same time—which is what actually happens when we make a sound like the EE in "meet." One tone comes from the back part of the throat, and the other comes from the channel that is created between the tongue and the roof of the mouth.[2]

Overtones can be created by deliberately adjusting the jaw and altering the mouth cavities. This is a technique that can be taught and learned, but the "indefinable quality" described by the Tibetan abbot happens for me unconsciously when I am in an alpha state of deep trance or meditation, or when I am seized with inspiration or passion, and my throat opens up and my breath seems to go on forever. For me, this is the ultimate expression of the holographic song.

Mantra. Mantras are words or sounds that are made inwardly, that reverberate silently upon the spiritual body as they are repeated during meditation. These words or sounds need not have any intellectual meaning. They are often Sanskrit words which have a high vibratory, astrological, numerological and psychological potency. The most well-known of these sounds is OM or AUM. All Names of God can be used as a mantra, including the biblical I AM THAT I AM.

Sufi Master Hazrat Inayat Kahn comments:

No doubt there is great value in the fact that millions of people have been clinging to these Mantras, repeating them day after day perhaps all their life and never becoming tired of doing so....

This shows us that beneath the repetition of words a mystery is hidden; and the day when man has fathomed it he will have discovered a great secret of life.[3]

Where to Tone. The beneficial effects of toning will increase if the air you're breathing is fresh. One way to do this is to tone outdoors. Another way is to leave the door or the windows open, or at least to air out the house before you begin. (Assuming that the outdoor air is reasonably fresh.)

If you want to feel totally comfortable doing the exercises described in this book, find a place where you can make noise without having to worry about disturbing housemates, family or neighbors. Wait until you are either alone or with a sympathetic person before attempting these exercises for the first time. Sounds that are new and unfamiliar can be distressing or annoying to others. When you release emotions through toning, you may find yourself starting to relive a traumatic incident, and the sounds you make could frighten someone who isn't prepared for them.

You may want to warn your closest neighbors that they might at times hear strange noises coming from your place. Tell them it's a form of therapy, and not to be alarmed (unless it's in the middle of the night).

There are other alternatives. Many people like to make sounds while they're driving. This is all right for routine exercises, but not advisable for exercises that could become highly emotional—unless you're driving on a country road where you can easily pull off. Nor is it advisable to listen to my Toning Meditation tape while driving; many people find that it puts them into a kind of trance. Other possible places to tone might be on the beach, or in the woods, or wherever you can be alone and away from people.

Alternately, you can tone under your breath. I have toned while sitting alongside someone, and they had no idea that I was toning—especially if there was some background noise, such as a car motor, or the sound of children, or music in the background. This is not nearly as effective as toning out loud, but it can be useful.

Another option is to go swimming and make your sounds under water.

You'll be able to hear muffled sounds, but people a short distance away will not.

If you need to use toning for emotional release and you simply cannot find a place where you can make loud sounds, have a pillow handy and scream into the pillow. Alternately, do a silent scream. Open your mouth and breathe out, with the same vehemence that you would put into a scream, but don't allow the sound to come out. This can be surprisingly satisfying.

Finding someone to work with. Some of the exercises in this book are designed for working with others, either making sounds for them, or encouraging them to make sounds. It's usually difficult to open up and make strange noises in front of someone else—even someone we love and trust. Just because we love someone doesn't mean that they're going to want to hear us making sounds, or that they're going to feel safe about making sounds themselves. Toning bypasses the intellect and goes directly to the emotions, so it makes us feel vulnerable. If someone you love doesn't want to hear you toning or doesn't choose to do these exercises with you, try not to take it personally .

If you're going to be sounding for someone else, be sure that whomever you work on is open-minded and receptive to this work and willing to release their emotions. Ideally, find a friend who is also interested in working with the voice, and then practice on each other.

Working with Children. Small children have an innate understanding of toning; they usually love it and learn rapidly. As they grow older, children may have an aversion to some of the sounds. Teenagers may be critical, since they are under so much peer pressure to conform.

Counselors and therapists working with children find that these exercises can be extremely effective for overcoming a child's natural shyness, for releasing pent-up emotions, and as an opener for meaningful communications.

A toning session might last from half an hour to two hours, and it could include any of the exercises in this book. In the beginning, start out with short sessions of about half an hour, using just one or two exercises from this chapter. If you wish, you can build up to one hour or longer sessions, but do so gradually so you can get used to using your voice in this way. The first exercise, *Warming and Stretching Your Voice*, is an excellent way to begin any toning session.

As you read through this book, you will decide which exercises best meet your needs, and you can choose the ones you feel most comfortable with. Comfort is usually a good guide, though sometimes it's rewarding to try something you distinctly *don't* want to do; it may be the key to releasing an emotion or memory that has been deeply suppressed.

Before doing any of the exercises in this book, please read the "Guidelines" in Chapter Ten on Emotional Release, so you'll know how to cope with physical and emotional reactions that may arise.

Now—it is time to begin!

Exercise: Warming and Stretching Your Voice

This is a great way to begin your day and to wake up your voice. It is ideal for beginning any toning session.

Spend three to five minutes repeatedly making the lowest sound you can make, using the tone E as in "red." Each time you make this tone, hold it for as long as you can. Between tones, inhale and take in as much air as possible. Feel your abdomen expanding as you inhale through your nose. After you've done this for a minute or two, make a conscious attempt to give *more* energy to your sound, making it forceful without straining your voice.

Spend another three to five minutes repeatedly toning the highest sound you can make, using the sound EE as in "tree." Each time you make this tone, hold it as long as possible. Again, after you've done this for a minute or two, make a conscious attempt to give *more* energy to your sound, making it forceful without straining your voice.

This is a good way to wake up your voice when you get out of bed, or when you're taking a shower in the morning. When you become accustomed to doing this simple exercise, you won't have to think about it; you can do it while you're walking around the house, washing dishes or driving to work. Without much effort, this exercise will help you to expand your lung capacity so you can breathe more deeply and hold your notes longer, while it gently expands the range and intensity of your voice.

Exercise: Roar Like a Tiger

This exercise is a great way to get over your inhibitions. Most of us have been taught to keep quiet; even as children, we were rarely encouraged to be creative, silly and emotional with our voices. Now's your chance!

If you want to touch your soul, start by touching your feelings. The feelings take us directly to the soulful right side of the brain. There is no better way to touch the feelings than through direct uninhibited sound.

Don't forget to use your body. Just try to howl like a dog while sitting with your chin tilted down. You'll find that you have to tilt your head back, exactly the way a dog howls at the moon, to get a really impressive howl. Your voice resides within your body, and it requires the uninhibited free movement of your body for its fullest expression.

One of the best ways to get over your inhibitions and start using your body together with your voice is to make animal sounds and movements. The ability of animals to emote directly through sound is something we would do well to imitate. American Indians imitate animals during their dances and rituals. Tai Chi and Yoga are ancient Chinese and Indian exercises for health and longevity, many of which are based on the observation of the movements of animals.

This exercise includes loosening up the muscles of your face. Like the voice, the face can express a wide range of emotions, but most of us have learned not to "betray" our feelings through facial expressions. It is difficult to tone or sing with a stiff face.

First, write down the names of ten animals that make sounds. Do this rapidly without thinking or analyzing.

Put your list aside and yawn. Open your mouth as far as it will go and shut your eyes tight. Open your eyes wide and stick out your tongue as far as it will go. Make a funny or ugly face. Get your body into it. Get down on all fours. Snarl and bare your teeth and arch your back.

Now look at your list (or have your partner read it aloud to you) and act out one animal at a time, making the noise for that animal at least three times, and using your whole body to make these sounds. The less inhibited you can become, the more fun you'll have and the more you will awaken your breath and voice.

As you can imagine, this is an exercise that children enjoy. If your friends are uninhibited, it can be a good party game.

Note: Sometimes the sound of a particular animal will evoke extremely deep feelings. If this happens, allow yourself to experience the feelings. If it brings up memories, let them come. Make the sound again and again until it no longer has a charge on it.

Sometimes a person will find that he or she has an extreme reluctance to make the sound of a particular animal. If this is so, and if you've been able to make other animal sounds, then you may have had a painful experience with this kind of animal. Be gentle with yourself. You may want to have someone there for support. Try to let the sound come out so that you can explore your past and release those old emotions.

Exercise: Following Your Intuition

When you allow your inner impulse to guide your voice, you'll be overcome by a desire to make sounds that seem to emerge from within. You'll know just what sounds to make, when to make them, and for how long. As you develop this ability, you'll find that healing with sound will come naturally to you.

Once you give yourself permission, you may find the desire to make sounds emerging with a spontaneous urgency at unpredictable times. If the timing or the place seems inappropriate to your conscious mind, there may be a hidden reason that your intuitive mind is tapping into. If the risk is not too great, it may be rewarding to trust that inner, intuitive voice and take the leap.

If you're with others, you might begin by saying, "I feel the desire to make a sound. Do you mind?"

The best way to develop this ability is to pay attention to your instincts. Whenever you have a "feeling" that you should take your umbrella, or that you should call your mother, or that you should stop at your friend's house on the way to work ... do it! It doesn't matter how irrational it may seem. Do it anyway. And keep a chart. (See Illustration.) The following exercise was taken from my book, *Color and Crystals.*

Keep track of every time you have a feeling about something. Write down whether or not you followed that feeling and the results. Then check either "Positive" or "Negative." Positive points indicate a positive vote for following your intuition. Negative points indicate a negative vote for following your intuition.

If you followed your intuition and you're glad you did, count this as a positive. If you didn't follow your intuition and you wish you had, count this as a positive. If you followed your intuition and you wish you hadn't, count this as a negative. If you didn't follow your intuition and you're glad you didn't, this is also a negative.

Judging from the results that my clients and students have had with this technique, I predict that about nine out of ten times that

Date	Feeling	Follow Through	Results	Pos.	Neg.
10/12	take umbrella	I didn't	it rained, got wet	✓	
10/25	drive to next town to buy shoes on sale	I did	they weren't on sale, wasted gas & time		✓
10/30	buy extra groceries on the way home	I did	husband brought friends home from work for dinner	✓	
11/2	talk to Alice about her son's school problems	I did	she was grateful	✓	
11/15	wash & vacuum car	I did	husband's father needed a ride to town	✓	
11/29	stop letting cat into house	I did	new roomate is allergic to cats	✓	
12/3	take extra tampons on trip	I did	period started early	✓	
12/5	write sweet note to my husband	I did	he came home early and my note cheered him up	✓	

Chart for following your intuition

you follow your intuition, you'll be glad you did. And nine out of ten times that you don't follow it, you'll wish you had.

In the beginning, you may confuse an intuitive impulse with a wish, fear or guilty thought. You might not know whether the urge to call your mother is coming from an inner knowing that she needs your help, or from a nagging sense of guilt that you *ought* to call her. (What we call conscience is NOT intuition.)

Until you learn to make these subtle distinctions (and it's just a matter of time, though you may never get it perfectly right), you simply have to put up with a slight margin of error. But be careful. Your intellect is accustomed to being in charge and may feel threatened when you begin giving power to your intuition. Your intellect is liable to pounce upon that one out of ten times and say "Aha! I told you so! You can't trust yourself!"

However, when you think about it, nine times out of ten is pretty good. If your intellect could do that, it would consider itself brilliant. One thing you can say for the intellect is that it's reasonable. That's why you need the chart. Then you can calmly point out to the intellect that the odds are good.

The next thing the intellect needs is a nice easy chair. It's been working too hard. Help it to relax and realize that it doesn't have to be in charge all the time. Consider the difference between hierarchical and tribal organization. Hierarchical government has one person in charge, whereas tribal organization usually has a group of people in charge: the war chief, the chief of agriculture, the medicine man or woman, and so forth.

Body, mind, heart and intuition function much better in the tribal mode. Once the mind understands this, it will often cooperate and allow the body, heart and spirit to take over when appropriate. One of my clients did extensive work on this and finally announced that his intuition was going to make the decisions and his intellect would implement them. This is an intelligent way to proceed.[4]

Exercise: Improvising on Words

This can be a great ice-breaker at a party—if your friends enjoy playing. And it's wonderful to do with children, or in mixed groups of adults and children.

Make a list of twenty to fifty words, including some animal words, some words that describe emotions, and some nonsense words. Don't think about it. This should be a stream-of-consciousness activity (non-rational). If you're doing this with a partner, your partner can write down the words for you. If you're doing it with a group, go around the circle once or twice and ask each person to call out one word, and have someone write down the words.

If you're doing this alone, the words may come easily, but some people can't think of anything and find themselves just looking around the room and naming objects that they see. If this happens with more than a few words, close your eyes and notice what words pop into your head and write these down. Here's a list of words that one fun-loving group came up with: what?, nose, hoo-ma, hushama, mist, eeii, hi, poop, bananas, monkeys, Buddha, sneeze, lions, zoo, ouch, growl.

When you feel satisfied that your list is complete, you're ready to begin toning. Stand up and make a sound for each word; give a kind of background or mood music or emphasis or sound expression for each word. (Examples: If the word is baby, you might feel like crying or screaming or going goo-goo. If the word is cat you might feel like growling or purring. If the word is gold you might feel inspired to make a high hymnal sound or a mellow full-bodied sound.) If it's a nonsense word, you'll have to let your imagination go wild to create a movement that "feels like" the sound.

If you're working with a partner, you may be tempted to explain what you're doing. ("This is the sound of the airplane going through the wind.") Don't explain; just do it for yourself. Sound is very powerful. You will find that if you let go of your inhibitions and get out of your rational mode, you can convey *a lot* through the power of your voice. Be sure to move around and use your face and your body to give full expression to your sounds.

Exercise: Toning with Children

This is a wonderful game to play with one or more children, and it's great to do while walking or riding in a car, plane or train. (*Roar Like a Tiger* and *Improvising on Words* are also great exercises for kids.)

The leader makes a sound and repeats it, a total of three times. The child (or children) imitate the sound as best they can, three times. Then it's the next person's turn to make a sound, three times, and everyone will imitate it as best they can, three times.

Start out with simple vowel sounds (A, EE, OO) and don't hold them too long. Then progress to more complex or silly sounds, and hold them a bit longer (moo, glue, poo, blah). Explain that the whole sound has to be held on one note, so if it's a word, it can't be a word with more than one syllable (dog is okay; dog-gie has two syllables and won't work). Nonsense sounds and syllables are just fine.

Children are likely to get excited while playing this game, and tend to become raucous, making all kinds of outrageous sounds. You may feel tempted to try and limit their expression to reasonably pleasant sounds. But if you can rejoice in their growing ability (and your own) to release tension and express feelings through sound, then you will probably find that you, too, are soon making ridiculous sounds and laughing and screaming, and acting very silly, which will be a wonderful source of release and pleasure to all of you.

8

HEALING WITH SOUND

The use of sound for healing was known to virtually every ancient culture, including the Egyptians, Greeks, Chinese, Persians, Hindus, Buddhists, Tibetans, Polynesians, Africans and American Indians. In western medicine, we are now using ultrasound to observe babies in utero; ultrasonic measurements can show the fetal heart size to predict congenital heart defect;[1] mammograms are used to detect breast cancer; chiropractors use ultrasound to speed the healing of tendons and joints, and ultrasound is used by sexologists in Sweden to determine which sexual positions are most likely to lead to orgasm.[2] There are a wide variety of devices to synchronize the two hemispheres of the brain through a combination of flashing lights, music and tones, for relaxation and stress reduction.

Sound affects our health in a variety of ways. Scientists have shown that sound variations of pitch, intensity and timbre can produce changes in the circulation of blood, and the blood pressure will go up or down when the medulla oblongata is stimulated by sound.[3]

We can understand the emotional impact of sound and its effect upon the body when we realize that the vagus nerve, which passes through the ear, extends into the larynx (the voice box) and all of the internal organs including the entire intestinal tract, back muscles, lungs and heart. It carries the fibers that control the release of gastric and pancreatic secretions, and inhibitory fibers of the heart.[4]

By 1926, research showed that music increases metabolism, changes muscular energy, increases respiration, and establishes physiological changes that correlate with emotional shifts. Contemporary work by ethnomusicologists showed physiological and physical changes in relation to vocal tones and rhythms.[5]

Apparently, sound is a kind of food for the brain and the entire body. Just to remain awake, the brain requires three billion stimuli per second for at least four and a half hours per day. Dr. Alfred Tomatis, French physician, psychologist and authority in auditory neurophysiology, explains how the ear charges the brain with electrical potential:

> The joints, the muscles, in other words, the body's posture—everything we use to fight against gravity—all this is tied to the labyrinth of the ear. It is the ear's vestibular labyrinth that keeps all these under control, which is balance. To this mechanism alone I believe we can credit 60% of the cortical charge. You also have, thanks to the energy of the sounds themselves, which is processed by the cochlea, a complementary charge of about 30%. Thus the ear accounts for from 90% to 95% of the body's total charge.[6]

Tomatis points out that the importance of using sound to charge the brain may be seen in the fact that the stapius muscle, which regulates one of the tiny bones of the middle ear, is the only muscle of the human body that never rests. Even the heart pulsates and thereby rests between each beat.[7]

The most important frequency range for charging the ear is between 2,000 and 4,000 cycles per second, which is the upper part of the speaking range. Dr. Tomatis explains that, "If your voice has good timbre, is rich in overtones, you are charging yourself each time you use it, and of course you are providing a benefit to whomever hears you!"

Tomatis became acutely aware of how important the voice is in charging the body when he was called to a Benedictine monastery in France. These monks ordinarily observed silence all day except for chanting from six to eight hours a day. The Benedictines are well known for working hard and sleeping little, and they eat a simple, mostly vegetarian diet. This French monastery had just been taken over by a new young abbot who was convinced that chant served no useful purpose, and had eliminated it. Within a short time, seventy out of ninety monks complained of feeling inexplicably fatiqued.

Doctors were called in and they tried to rectify the situation by prescribing more sleep, and by adding meat to the diet—only to make things worse. When Dr. Tomatis arrived, he promptly prescribed a return to their usual chanting schedule. Within five months, almost all of the monks were restored to health and vigor, resuming their usual intensive work schedule. According to Dr. Tomatis, many Catholic monasteries have closed in recent times, but the ones that practice the traditional Gregorian chant have remained open.[8]

Gregorian Chant is a collection of chants taken from various cultures and standardized into the Catholic mass by St. Gregory (Pope from 590-604 A.D.). It is different than ordinary music because the timing is not according to meter, but rather depends upon the ability of the singers to chant on a prolonged exhalation. The training takes four years before a novice is brought into the choir.[9]

Because the chant is based on the breath, it has a powerful effect on the listener, who soon finds him or herself taking deep breaths, which in turn slows down the heart and reduces blood pressure. Tomatis points out that, "If you put an oscilloscope on the sounds of Gregorian chant, you see that they all come within the bandwidth for charging the ear. There is not a single sound which falls outside of this."[6]

Many people use Gregorian Chants to calm them down, and to increase their energy, memory and concentration. I've found my recording of Gregorian Chants to be indispensible during the writing of this book. It keeps my mind calm and prevents my body from holding tension while working for long hours at the computer. Tomatis explains that music in relatively lower frequencies (like shamanic drumming) affects the more primitive areas of the brain, creating a hypnotic state, whereas the Gregorian Chant stimulates the cortex, making you feel alert.[10]

Let's look further at how sound affects the health of the body. Dr. Peter Guy Manners works with sound in his medical practice at Bretforton Hall Clinic in Worcester, England. He writes, "Experimentation indicates that human beings, as all objects, are radiating sound waves; therefore their fields are sonic fields."[11]

Lest this sound too vague and mystical, let's talk about animals. We know that animals are more sensitive to vibrations than people. Human chauvinism makes us think that reality can be defined only by what human beings experience with their five senses. It's difficult for us to believe that there are sounds we cannot hear and vibrations we cannot feel. Yet we all know that dogs and cats hear sounds that humans cannot hear. Farmers can tell when a storm is coming by watching the chickens; they feed heartily before a storm—even when there's no apparent sign of rain.

The seawater crocodile can sense electrical vibrations over 100 yards away. The shark has electrosensors covering its snout so it can pick up the vibrations of a creature hiding *under* the sand. Sharks have a hearing-feeling sense (scientists call it a "lateral line") that allows them to sense the vibrations of moving prey.[12]

Then it is safe to say that we are all vibrations, and every part of the body has its own vibration. Dr. Manners defines harmony within the body, and gives us our first clue about how to use sound to discover the source of bodily disharmony.

> Each individual has his own different pattern, or collection of tones just as each individual has a unique shape. We can see from this that harmony is the secret of perfect health. Within the human body any deviation from this harmony would result in ill health....

> We can easily see that each organ will have its own sonic (or sound) field. If properly detected this should provide information on processes going on in a particular organ. [13]

When we realize that each organ has its own sonic field, and that all the organs need to be in tune in order to create a harmonic whole, this gives us a greater understanding of what health and Vibrational Healing are all about. It also helps us to understand why an exercise like "Toning for the Organs" can actually affect the health of our internal organs.

Discoveries by Dr. Royal Rife in the 1930s give us a clear indication of just how potent the right tones can be for eliminating disease or disharmony from the body. Dr. Rife found that every cell has its own vibratory frequency, and every cell within a specific organ system has a similar vibratory resonance. Rife is best known for his amazing microscope that magnifies living cells at 100,000 magnifications. While observing the internal workings of a living human cell, he took a Ray-O-Vac tube and a frequency generator, and he charged the cells with different frequencies. Eventually he found a resonance that would explode the cells.

If there were a disease of a particular group of cells, he could find the specific frequency that would explode and remove the diseased cells. Armed with this knowledge, Rife started curing cancer. If there were cancer of the breast, he could take a biopsy and put it under the microscope and then observe the cells while he amped up his frequency generator until the cells exploded. Once he determined which frequency was required to obliterate the malignant cells, he would put the person next to the Ray-O-Vac tube, direct it to the breast, and after the treatment, the cancer cells would be gone without affecting the rest of the breast or the rest of the body.

Apparently certain powerful people thought that Rife's work was not in their best interest, and his laboratory was broken into, and all of his records and instruments were destroyed. Today there is one Rife Microscope at the Smithsonian Institute, and people are now attempting to reproduce his work in Germany, Canada, and elsewhere.[14]

Perhaps Rife's work inspired the development of the German lithotripter, which translates as "stone crusher." This remarkable medical machine destroys kidney stones by selectively attacking them with the appropriate sound resonance. The patient sits in a bath with the kidney area just above a "belt" through which explosions of sound are emitted, which mimic the sound frequency of the kidney stones. Gallstones are also being treated with the lithotripter.[15]

Rife's method and the lithotripter work by destroying unhealthy cells with sound. Dr. William Tiller, a Guggenheim Fellowship member from Stanford University, gives us a different concept of healing with sound. Tiller writes about providing cells with the sounds they need to make them healthy.

In *Radionics, Radiesthesia and Physics*, Tiller explains that each gland of the body has its own healthy waveform, so it is possible to scan the waveform of a gland to detect abnormalities. Once detected, "if energy having the normal or healthy waveform of the gland is pumped into ... the gland [it] will be driven in the normal or healthy mode." [16]

This helps us to understand why exercises in this chapter such as *Toning for the Pain in Your Body*, *Toning the Internal Organs* and *Toning with Bodywork* are effective. We can see that when parts of the body are diseased, the vibrations change. Toning is a way of bringing healthy waveforms into the glands and re-awakening healthy vibrations within the body.

Someone who is psychically sensitive can send out sounds, much as a bat uses radar, to scan the wavefield of each gland and check for imbalances. Using their intuition, this person can then find sounds to charge the glands with healthy energy, thereby restoring them to health.

Norman Cousins inspires us with yet another way of using sound for health, in the form of laughter. Laughter is a form of toning that was put to good use by the Zen master who told his students that if they would say "Ho! Ho!" vigorously for five minutes each day, they would never die. According to folk tradition, the renowned immortalist, Santa Claus, was well-known for his sage expression: "Ho! Ho! Ho!"

In *Anatomy of an Illness,* Cousins tells about his struggle with a rare life-threatening disease, ankylosing spondylitis. This illness is characterized by a gradual deterioration of collagen, a fibrous substance found in the connective tissue of every part of the body, including the spine.

Norman Cousins was familiar with Dr. Hans Selye's famous work on the physiological characteristics of stress, which shows that constant repeated stress and unpredictable but frequent stress lead to illness and disease. Cousins reasoned that if distress causes disease, then joy and laughter should cause healing. With that theory in mind, he arranged to have funny movies and hilarious old TV programs shown throughout the day in his hospital room. He was delighted to report that ten minutes of good belly-laughing gave him two hours of relief from pain. Eventually he cured his disease with laughter and massive doses of Vitamin C.[17] You, too, can use laughter and other enjoyable forms of toning to improve your physical, mental and emotional health.

Guidelines for Practitioners

Most of this book is directed toward self-healing, but all the exercises can be used in a client-practitioner context. It is useful to distinguish different forms of toning, and the practitioner's role in assisting the release of sound. In some of these exercises (like *Toning for the Pain in Your Body*), your clients may be unable to make their own sounds. Once you have become proficient at making these sounds for yourself, you may be able to scan their body with your voice and begin toning for them—which may trigger them into making their own tones.

There are three basic sounds: (1) cleansing and releasing, (2) soothing and relaxing and (3) regenerative. When sounds are released, memories tend to follow, so be prepared to do counseling in conjunction with this work (see Guidelines for Emotional Release in Chapter Ten).

Cleansing and Releasing. Sounds that express emotions help to release stress and tension. Moaning and groaning are cleansing sounds that come naturally when aches and pains are being released. Encourage your clients to make sounds, and offer to join them. Most people feel less self-conscious when they can hear someone else making outrageous sounds, and this helps to put them at ease so they can put more feeling into their sounds.

High-pitched, penetrating sounds, or even fierce screaming can help break up energy blockages that may have led to emotional and physical armoring. If you sense that a client is holding onto an emotional sound that he or she cannot get in touch with, you might say, "I feel the impulse to make a sound, and it may not be very pleasant. Is that all right?" If your client says yes, then you can add, "Feel free to join me."

Release the sound that you feel from within. It may be a blood-curdling, terrifying scream and your client may be amazed to find him or herself joining you. This could go on for several minutes, and it might actually end in laughter! Releasing a scream that has been held in for decades can be a joyous, liberating experience.

Another use of cleansing sounds occurs when there is negative energy in a room. Emotions such as anger, fear and sadness that are fully expressed and resolved do not leave negative energy in a room, but when people are angry and brooding and unable to release these heavy emotions, they tend to leave bits and pieces of negative energy behind them wherever they go. A dark cloud seems to hover in the energy field of the room, even after the person is gone. Sharp, intense sounds combined with sweeping gestures can work effectively to purge this energy and cleanse the room.

Soothing and relaxing. Soothing sounds help bring body and spirit back into their natural harmony and alignment. Through toning, you can provide a soothing environment for the release of tension. Humming can be calming to the nervous system, and may help your client to breathe deeply.

You may feel inspired to sing words of support and encouragement, or even to break into familiar bars of music or pop tunes. Trust the impulse; it often turns out to be surprisingly appropriate.

Regenerative. Sit in silence with your client and allow your energy to align with theirs, so that you can *feel* the resonance they are lacking. This may happen spontaneously while you are talking or while they are toning. Once you feel the resonance they need, allow your voice to provide that sound. When regenerative sounds are for survival or sexual issues, they tend to be low and full-bodied. When they are for self-worth and love, they tend to be in the mid range. When they are for opening to spirituality, they tend to be high and ethereal.

If the sounds are in alignment with your client's highest energy, your client may have physiological reactions including having tears come to their eyes; feeling a wave of heat rush over them; having their heart-beat slow down or increase; feeling a great weight lifted from their shoulders or feeling prickly sensations throughout their body.

Sometimes —particularly toward the end of a session—you may have an impulse to sing silly songs: popular songs, rock-n-roll, old-fashioned or sentimental songs. These often turn out to be just the right thing, and the laughter that follows may be the kind of support your client needs to lighten up and come back to their body.

Exercise: Laughing Your Way to Heath

According to Laurel Elizabeth Keyes, author of *Toning, The Creative Power of the Voice*, the "H" and "K" sounds such as "Hi, Hah, Hoh, Hu, Kah and Koo" stimulate the glandular system. They are produced by tightening the abdominal muscles and forcing the breath out against the roof of the mouth, which produces strong vibrations in the adrenal, thymus, pituitary and pineal glands. Laughter is usually thought of as a repetition of "h" sounds such as "ha-ha-ha" or "he-he-he."[15]

In the days of the great sailboats, a single sail weighed as much as two tons, and it would take more than twenty men to raise one sail. When it was time to hoist the sail, the men would chant in unison, "Heave Ho!" with each pull upon the ropes.

In my workshops, when the energy begins to wane, I'll have my students do the following exercise. The results are highly enlivening.

> Stand up with your feet shoulder-width apart. Stretch your hands up to the heavens and open your mouth and yawn. Lean over and try to touch your toes. Begin at your feet and slap your body to enliven it, moving up your legs and up your torso until you are beating on your chest, and then bring your fists up into the air with your arms straight and throw your hands wide open. While you are doing this, make a sustained HEY sound, beginning in the low register, and as you move up your body, bring the sound gradually up into a high tone until you release the sound explosively.

Stand tall and say the following in a strong declarative manner:
HEY-HEE-HI-HO-HU!

(A simple way to remember this is that you're just adding a vowel after each "H": A-E-I-O-U.)

Repeat three times.

Thanks to Laurel Elizabeth Keyes for inspiring this exercise.

Exercise: Toning for the Pain in Your Body

Stand with your legs about shoulder length apart and your body relaxed. If you prefer, sit at the edge of a chair with your back straight and then you can stand up and move around when the energy gets moving.

Inhale through your nose and draw the breath down to your abdomen so you can actually see your abdomen rising. Exhale through your mouth, making a low moan, or whatever comes naturally. Do this ten times.

If you have a specific pain that needs attention, proceed to the "Instructions" section below. If the pain feels more general, the following will be helpful.

Continue to breathe deeply while you mentally scan your body, starting at your feet and going to the top of your head. You are looking for areas of tightness, pain, tension, extremes of hot or cold, or anything that feels abnormal. You can do this any way you like, but if you need instructions, you can proceed as follows:

Move your attention fairly rapidly over your entire body. Begin by scanning your back, including:

feet	small of your back
ankles	area between your
calves	shoulder blades
knees	shoulders
thighs	upper arms
buttocks	elbows
anus	lower arms
tailbone	wrists
lower back	hands

Then scan the front of your body, including

genitals	lungs
women: vagina,	neck
uterus, tubes, ovaries	jaw
men: penis, scrotum,	lips and mouth
prostate gland	tongue
large intestines	throat
small intestines	nose and cheeks
stomach	temples and ears
liver (under right	eyebrows and eyes
rib cage)	forehead
spleen (under left	brain
rib cage)	top of head
heart	

Instructions: Wherever you feel pain, tension or some abnormal feeling, bring your attention there and consciously breathe into it. As you exhale, release tension from that part of your body. Now you can do the verbal technique described below, or proceed directly to the sound technique.

1) Verbal. Observe the energy as you exhale and describe the way it feels out loud. (Example: John has a pain in his shoulders. "I feel a tightness in my shoulders.")

Continue breathing and describe the pain or tension in greater detail, using metaphors. (Example: "My shoulders feel all scrunched together. It reminds me of cartoons where the character is very 'up tight.' " "It feels like I'm carrying the whole world on my shoulders.")

2) Sound. Give a sound to the feeling. If the sound doesn't come spontaneously, begin by toning as low as you can and slowly raise the pitch until you find a tone that resonates with the pain. Continue making sounds until you feel a release, as if you've given yourself an inner massage. (Example: John sticks his tongue out and says, "yech" on a sustained sound, as if he were going to vomit. Then he makes an abrupt, ugly sound, as if he were pushing someone away. Taking a deep breath, he makes a loud "bah" sound. He smiles with satisfaction, throws up his arms and with upraised voice he flings "bah" into the air, with a sense of celebration and liberation.

John shakes his shoulders and rolls his head on his neck, making a powerful O sound while opening his arms in a gesture of open embrace. "My shoulders feel much better," he declares, with evident satisfaction and surprise.)

Repeat this process for every pain or discomfort in your body.

There are many ways this exercise can unfold. Ron had severe chronic low back pain. He went directly to part two and began toning on a low hum, moving his hips, swaying back and forth. After about five minutes, his tone raised and got a little louder as he began twisting his body gently from side to side. This continued for another five minutes and then the tone raised again and he started moving his arms and flexing his back. After several minutes of this, the tone moved yet higher as he rolled his head and raised his shoulders. The tones seemed to gravitate between mild release and nurturing vibration. He commented later that at one point the sound reminded him of a chainsaw. He said the pain was like being stabbed in the back. Tears came to his eyes as he remembered being beaten by his father when he was eight years old because he didn't want to use the chainsaw.

Ron was amazed to find his body moving painlessly in ways that he hadn't been able to move for years. When he finished, he felt much looser and the pain was definitely diminished. Days later he still felt a significant improvement in his back.

———————

Here's how Margaret experienced this exercise. She arrived looking old and miserable. She told me that she thought she was falling in love—with another woman. She always thought of herself as being bisexual, but she had never had a love affair with a woman. She was suffering from severe pain at the back of her chest, which is the hidden part of the heart chakra, or love center.

When she did this exercise, she made a sound for her back. It was shaky and deep. "I'm afraid of getting into this," she admitted. With the next exhale, we could hear one of her vertebrae pop. This is not unusual; she had given her spine an adjustment just by sounding and acknowledging her fear.

As she exhaled again, she released an AH sound and rotated her shoulders, expanding her chest, and another vertebra popped. She had no idea that she was making the sound that corresponds to the heart chakra. "I'm up-tight," she observed.

She returned to her back, behind her chest, and made more "scary" sounds, like in a fun house, after which she giggled and then burped, releasing a considerable amount of gas. (It's common to hold tension in the gut. As the tension is released, belching often occurs.)

Margaret found a low note, which she toned repeatedly, finding it soothing. She opened her mouth wide, dropping her jaw, and stretched her arms in front of her. She pulled back from the elbows, expanding her shoulders and opening her chest, while making expansive opening sounds.

Standing up, she rotated her hips, freeing the energy at her pelvis, making tribal sounds. She started gyrating her pelvis and said she was feeling sexy, but she felt pain at her tailbone. I picked up a drum and she broke into a wild, erotic dance, arching her back, thrusting her pelvis, throwing up her arms and gyrating her hips while making rhythmic deep gutteral sounds.

Finally she broke into gales of laughter and collapsed on the floor. She looked so relaxed—ten years younger than when she walked in the door. She said she was looking forward to seeing her friend again and felt excited about the possibility that they might become lovers.

Exercise: Toning the Internal Organs

This exercise can be used for general tonification of the internal organs, which include the heart, lungs, kidneys, stomach, spleen, liver, small and large intestines. It can also be used to energize the endocrine glands, which include the pituitary, thyroid, parathyroid, adrenals, ovaries, testes, and islands of Langerhans in the pancreas. It may also be a way of locating weakness and imbalance in the organs and glands, releasing the old energy and replacing it with healthy new energy.

The exercise is divided into three parts: (1) finding and expressing the imbalance or illness in the organ(s); (2) releasing the blocks, and (3) harmonizing the energy. The following exercise focuses on the lungs, but it can be used for any organ or gland—in fact, it can be used anywhere on the body. After you learn the basic technique, modify the exercise to meet your needs.

1) Finding and expressing the imbalance or illness in the organ(s). Bring your attention to one of your internal organs. Observe how it feels. Use several words to describe the feeling. Let the words come spontaneously, without judging or censoring them, even if they seem silly.

Make a sound that expresses each of these words. Repeat the sound at least three times.

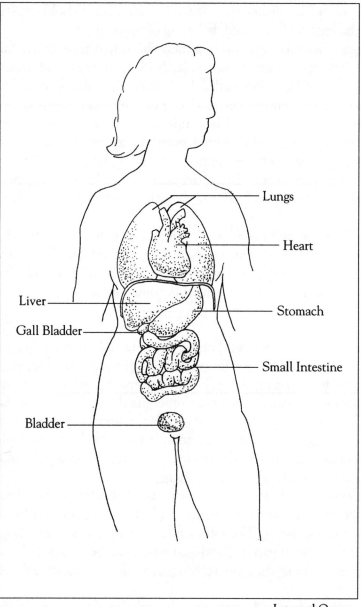

Internal Organs

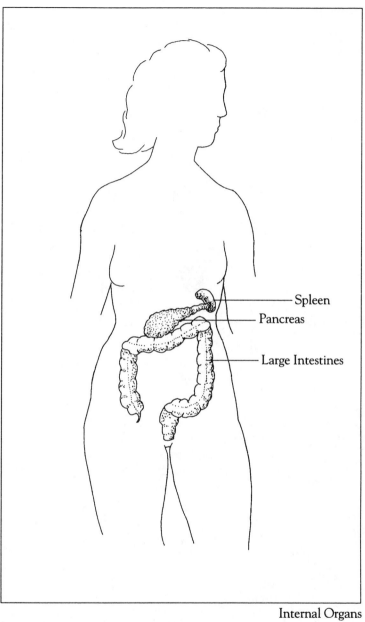

Spleen

Pancreas

Large Intestines

Internal Organs

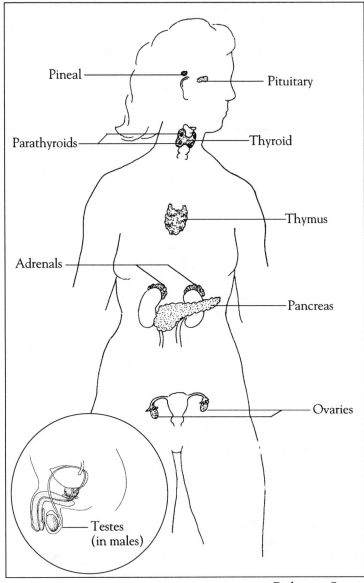

Pineal

Pituitary

Parathyroids

Thyroid

Thymus

Adrenals

Pancreas

Ovaries

Testes
(in males)

Endocrine System

Example: George had adult-onset asthma, which had been getting progressively worse for the past ten years. He described his lungs as "tight, damp, cold, wheezy, breezy, sneezy." When I asked him to express the tightness of his lungs, George made a series of short, tight little sounds. He felt silly and self-conscious, but I urged him to be uninhibited and playful. For the dampness, he stuck out his tongue and made some more short little sounds. For the coldness, he made shivering sounds. For the wheeziness, he made short wheezy sounds. By this time, he had to stop to blow his nose. For the breeziness, he pursed his lips and made breathy sounds. For the sneeziness, he made little sneezes.

    2) Releasing the blocks. Close your eyes. Go back to the first feeling-word you used. Find a sound that resonates with that feeling. If it doesn't emerge spontaneously, make a low sound and then go progressively higher until you find a sound that seems to express the feeling. As the sound merges with the feeling, both the sound and the feeling will change, helping to release the emotional blocks that were holding the old feeling in place. Keep toning as the feeling and the sound change from discordant to harmonious. This may take one or more sessions to accomplish.

George found a sound that seemed to resonate with the tightness. He used that sound repeatedly, until he could feel the tightness opening up and relaxing. As the tightness in his lungs relaxed, the sound became increasingly more sustained and open. We did the same with each of the other symptoms. This took about five minutes.

    3) Harmonizing the energy. Tune in on the whole organ, and all of the feelings you have described. Get the whole picture. Then make sounds that convey the overall feeling in your organ, emphasizing any negative or unpleasant energies that you feel at the site of the organ. Don't be afraid to make ugly, disgusting or angry sounds. Remember that you are literally cleansing your inner body with sound. Every emotion that is rejected and repressed by your conscious mind gets stored within your body, where it eventually leads to discomfort and disease. So every emotion that you can express with your voice becomes a liberated feeling that no longer needs to hide. Keep sounding until the sound becomes pleasant and harmonious and you feel finished. This may take a minute or twenty minutes, or it may require many sessions.

As George toned for his lungs, he discovered that he had a full, pleasant voice and could sustain a tone for a surprisingly long time. When we finished the session, he was breathing freely. That night he didn't have to use his chest inhaler, which he found quite amazing; ordinarily he had to wake up several times during the night to use it.

Thanks to Swami K.M. Tayumanavar for inspiring this exercise.

Exercise: Toning with Bodywork

It is a joy to give yourself permission to make sounds while you are giving or receiving a massage, or any kind of body work. This section is directed to the masseuse, though similar instructions apply to other kinds of body workers (including those doing acupressure, reflexology, Rolfing and other kinds of deep tissue work, etc.). The person receiving body work will also benefit from reading this.

Please review the Guidelines For Practitioners in this chapter and the Guidelines For Emotional Release in Chapter Ten. There are three basic sounds: (1) cleansing and releasing, (2) soothing and relaxing and (3) regenerative. Sounds may be released in the usual way, or—if you want the sound to enter a particular part of the body—you can cup your hands to create a kind of echo chamber, put your mouth up to your cupped hands and tone directly into the body. Some practitioners prefer to tone with their lips barely touching the body or to tone through the clothing, or through a piece of cloth that has been placed on the body.

To clarify how body work and sounding can be combined with counseling and other modalities, I'll give some examples of how I have used sound in this way.

Ted came to me because he had a serious case of lethargy and depression. Ordinarily I would begin by encouraging him to talk about what had been happening in his life, particularly events preceding the feelings of depression. On this occasion, he had barely started talking when I had an impulse to press on his stomach. Asking for and receiving his permission, I started kneading the area around his solar plexus. Following my intuition, I found myself making gagging sounds, pushing firmly on his abdomen and gagging repeatedly (cleansing and releasing).

Ted broke into intense heaving sighs and released a well of tears (his own cleansing and releasing). "I've been feeling nauseous lately," he explained. "While you were working on me, I realized that I was feeling sick to my stomach about my family situation." He explained that his grown son wanted to come and live with him. There was plenty of room in the house, but it felt like an invasion of his privacy. Once he got in touch with his gut feelings about the situation, he realized that he wanted to make other arrangements with his son.

I asked him to lie down and I placed my hand gently on his solar plexus, directing blue light to the area as I toned UU several times (soothing and relaxing). Then I directed yellow light to the same area as I toned AOM (regenerative). (See Chapter Ten on *Color Breathing*.)

When I saw him two weeks later, he said he had a great talk with his son, and it felt good to acknowledge his own needs, and his son seemed to respect him for that.

Another example of a cleansing sound happened recently, when my husband, Gordon, got a new weed-whacker and spent all afternoon enthusiastically whacking weeds and mowing the lawn. By the end of the day, the muscles in his right forearm were so traumatized that he could barely make a fist with his fingers, and his energy was totally depleted.

As I massaged his forearm, I began to make a high-pitched sound. While I was making the sound, I realized that I was unconsciously imitating the vibration of the weed whacker, and I could "feel" how the energy of the weed-whacker had come into his nerves. (This sound doesn't fall into the three categories; it was just a way of aligning myself with his energy.) Then I made a low, deep tone as an antidote, to calm his energy (soothing and relaxing). Within a few minutes, the pain was gone and much of his strength was restored. By morning, his arm was fine and he felt energetic.

Sounding can be combined with body work in a variety of ways, including conventional massage. If you want to start toning with bodywork, here is a simple way to begin.

> Find a friend who is open-minded. Offer to give your friend a massage in exchange for being able to experiment with sound. Before the massage, ask permission to make absolutely any sounds that you feel like making. Encourage your friend to do the same. When you finish the session, sit down and give each other feedback about how it felt to work together.

9

EMOTIONAL RELEASE THROUGH TONING

I studied with Dr. Elisabeth Kubler-Ross, the Swiss psychiatrist who did revolutionary work with death and loss. She is less well-known for her important work with teenagers, which involved going into high schools where the students had serious behavior problems, and persuading the School Boards to put in screaming rooms.

Kids go into these soundproof rooms that have mattressess on the floors and walls, and they beat on the mattresses and scream their heads off. After they've released all that aggression in the screaming room, they don't have to be aggressive with other kids. When they can release their emotional and physical pain, they no longer need to numb themselves with drugs and alcohol.

These reactions are not limited to teenagers. When we are in stressful situations, we start pumping adrenalin and other hormones for "fight or flight." That served us well in primitive times when we had to kill the enemy or run from attack. But in modern times, this is not acceptable behavior.

When you stifle your natural impulses, those hormones turn into toxins that get stored in your body and gradually build up to create chronic heart disease, arthritis, cancer and other debilitating diseases. I've helped innumerable people to re-live traumatic incidents from their childhood, and when they can scream and curse and hit the mat, these incidents come back with perfect clarity, as if they happened yesterday. The release of old repressed emotions enables them to experience a sense of anticipation and joy in life that they hadn't felt since they were infants. Then they can let go of chronic emotional pain that plagued them for years. It is amazing to see how the release of emotional pain leads directly into the release of physical pain. People find they are able to stop drinking and get off harmful medications when these old pains are released.

Toning is a remarkable way of letting go of emotions that have become trapped in specific parts of the body. It is also a way of restoring harmony so that the ailing part can find its natural interrelationship with the whole body, allowing the energy to flow freely.

There are men and women who rarely express their emotions, but at a tragic opera, when assaulted by the heart-rending cries of a dying heroine, the tears flow freely. Song is one way of releasing emotions, and tragic opera can be a wonderful emotional purge for those who are receptive to it.

Laeh Maggie Garfield describes it well in her fine book, *Sound Medicine*.

> ...opera buffs go to hear favorite singers not so much for their total performance but for the special notes they are known to hit during stressfully written arias. Most often the operatic devotee awaits the high pitch of the dramatic soprano, who unknowingly strikes a healing chord for the rapt listener. The fan is thereby revitalized by the evening's performance.[1]

99

American opera-lovers prefer to hear their favorite operas in a foreign tongue rather than be distracted by the words, so they can focus on the delicious intensity of emotion conveyed by the power of the voice.

As the preverbal infant so eloquently demonstrates, sounds can express every nuance of human emotion. If young children are not repressed, you can see in them a perfect demonstration of the art of emotional release through sounding. When a child is sad, he or she will cry, wail, or moan. When a child is happy, he or she will sing, shout and giggle.

All of these sounds may be distressing to adults who seek to create a harmonious atmosphere. Since most of us are constantly being bombarded by sounds that we cannot control, it's natural to want to eliminate the ones that we *can* control. Since we're obviously bigger than our children, it's tempting to tell them to be quiet.

On the other hand, it is damaging to suppress a child's natural emotional expression. This doesn't mean that children should be encouraged to yell and scream and be inconsiderate of others. But there are times when emotional outbursts are appropriate, and hopefully a discerning adult will be able to recognize such times.

A wide variety of new therapies have emerged to help adults relive incidents from their childhood when they were not allowed to express their emotions. Sounding is one of these techniques. If children are allowed to release emotions through sound and movement, it can contribute to their emotional, mental and physical health—as the following story will clearly illustrate.

Alana and her twelve-year-old daughter, Lizzy, were driving home on a Friday night. Coming around the bend on the freeway, they saw a car about a half block ahead of them, making a dangerous U-turn in the middle of the road. The car was unable to complete the turn and Alana crashed into it.

Checking to see that neither she nor Lizzy were hurt, Alana got out of her car, still shaking from the shock and the impact, and went to the man to see if he was all right. Fortunately, there were no casualties, but both cars were demolished.

Alana felt proud of her composure as she waited for the police to arrive, trying to comfort poor Lizzy, who was sobbing uncontrollably. When the police drove up and started questioning Alana, Lizzy ran into the field alongside the car, screaming and hollering. It was extremely annoying to Alana, but she was committed to allowing her daughter to express her feelings—as long as she wasn't doing anything to harm anyone.

They got a ride home, and one hour after the accident, Lizzy returned to normal. Alana, on the other hand, discovered that she had severe whiplash in her left shoulder. This pain continued for months, until she came to me. I used light hypnosis to help her relive the accident, and she finally touched the true source of her pain: the utter fear of losing her child, and her life. I encouraged her to express this fear in sound, and she belted out a scream of sheer terror.

Through screaming, Alana was finally able to express and release her emotional pain, and the old program of having to brace herself for the impact. Her body had become frozen in a posture of tension since the powerful message she had sent to her muscles and tissues was to be in a state of ready alertness. The scream was a message to her subconscious mind that the impact had, in fact, occurred, and now it was time to release.

The whiplash pain diminished over the next two weeks. If Alana had not been so civilized, she might have followed her daughter's example and released the pain immediately—or when she came home from the accident—and saved herself months of suffering.

———————

Chava Lasson describes the harmful effects of preventing children from expressing their emotions in her book, *Am I Laughing Too Loud?*

Depending upon the personality, children will react to restrictions to making sounds in different ways. Some will rebel, resist, persist, while others will withdraw, keep their voices muted or clam up altogether. Whatever the reaction, a neurotic pattern has been established resulting in the distortion of the voice. A bully will grow up to have a coarse, aggressive voice, while the easily subdued child will have to be asked to speak more loudly as he matures.

Take a destructive child, give him an opportunity to restructure his energy and you will have a peaceful, creative human being. Joshua was the four-year-old terror in the nursery school where I taught. One day when he was behaving abominably, I took him into an empty room where I had brought a drum. He ran to it, played it, turned it upside down, and said, "I killed my enemies." His aggressiveness gradually spent itself and he began to explore the potential sounds of the drum. He stood on it and gave me a sly look to see if I would stop him. When I did nothing he proceeded to jump up and down on the head of the drum, doing what looked like a tribal dance, singing and waving his hands and shouted, "My hands are barefooted." Then he sat on the drum and sang, "I am a sitter, I sit on my head."

He was very calm after this session and chose the quiet involvement of painting and playing with the clay.

When energy is freed, with sound playing an important part, it opens the doors to creativity and beckons the latent artist to emerge.[2]

Chava is an eighty-three-year-old voice and toning teacher who lives and works in Los Angeles. She is one of my teachers, and her book inspired me to bring sound to a pain in my right hip. Since I have had plenty of experience with emotional release, I soon found myself howling and writhing on the floor in utterly excruciating pain as I relived having my leg crushed between two cars, an event that happened over a year before.

I screamed at the top of my lungs and grabbed my leg and fell over, just exactly as I did during the accident. When the accident occurred, I probably would have continued screaming for about fifteen minutes if the police and the ambulance driver hadn't arrived and needed to question me. Reliving this incident and giving myself permission to scream for as long as I wanted, helped my whole body to complete a cycle of shock and pain.

Through screaming, I was able to re-experience the fear that I might lose my leg, that I might never walk or bike or run again. Through screaming, I was able to express my anger at the man who backed into me and then drove away. Through this ten-minute vocal release of old, stored-up pain, I was able to instantly reduce the swelling in my hip by more than half, and the pain was almost totally gone. By giving myself permission to fully express my rage, I released the pain that no amount of physical therapy, massage or acupuncture had been able to touch.

Sound can be used as a form of deep tissue work, to release old programs and pain that we have stored in specific parts of our bodies. The implications of how sound can be used for healing are enormous.

Anna was an emotionally withdrawn and extremely overweight teenager. When she was feeling especially depressed, she found it comforting to turn on rock music. The worse she felt, the louder she turned up the music.

Rock stars are best loved when they are most outrageous. They wear crazy costumes, paint themselves wildly, do strange things to their hair, act out with blatantly childish behavior, and make loud, raucous music. They do everything that a teenager's parents tell them not to do.

We live in a spectator society, where most of us grow up watching television instead of getting out and living our lives. We watch others play sports instead of playing sports ourselves. We get others to pray for us instead of praying for ourselves. Most of us expect others to think for us instead of thinking for ourselves. And there are ways in which we get others to express our feelings instead of expressing them ourselves.

I taught Anna how to tone, and she was finally able to express the pain she felt at being emotionally abandoned by her mother. Once she gave herself permission to scream and yell, she no longer needed the rock stars to do it for her. As she released the pain, the sound went from meek to strong and full, and she was amazed by the power of her own voice. Over the next few sessions, her voice grew stronger, and she noticed herself becoming more assertive, demonstrative and outgoing. She lost the compulsive need to keep feeding her face and stuffing down her emotions, and she dropped forty pounds in two months. Though she still enjoyed certain rock stars, she had no more interest in listening to intensely loud music.

Kate worked with young retarded children during the day, and at night she was the single mother of two young children. She loved her work and she was a great mother, but having to meet the constant demands of her own children gave her no opportunity to unwind from the stress of the day. When Kate came to me, she was suffering from stiffness in her joints. Arthritis is a disease of hardening; i.e., it tends to occur when people harden themselves against other people or against their own feelings.

I had Kate start out with the *Warming and Stretching Your Voice* exercise in Chapter Eight. Since she worked with children, I thought she would enjoy *Roar Like a Tiger* (also in Chapter Eight)—which she did, with gusto. As she loosened up her voice, the depressed, middle-aged woman who had walked in the door turned into a bright, vibrant young woman who was enthusiastic about life and eager to have a good time.

"I have a very noisy old car," she mused, with a look of mischief in her eyes. "Do you suppose that it might help me if I could ... make car noises?"

I had no idea what she was talking about, but I encouraged her to try it out.

"Do you think I should do it *now?*" she asked, incredulously." I mean, it's going to sound really ridiculous..."

"Just tell your judge to sit in the back seat and be quiet," I reassured her.

She smiled and got down on all fours and started to make the most God-awful racket of coughs, spurts, vroom-vroom-vrooms, grating noises and loud bellowing sounds. She was crawling all over the room and having an absolutely marvelous time! After about five minutes of this, she collapsed on the floor, and by that time we were both laughing hysterically.

I let her rest for a few minutes, and then we came up with a plan. Every day after work she would take the long route home through the hills and do Car Noise Therapy. This would give her time to release the tension of the day. Then she would drive home.

Alice called me a month later and she was elated. "My joints don't hurt anymore! My kids like me better. I am feeling *so good*. Joy, this stuff really works!"

Guidelines for Emotional Release

Sound bypasses the intellect and has the inherent ability to trigger the emotions, so all of the exercises in this book may bring up deep feelings. The following exercises are specially designed to help you get in touch with your emotions.

You may have physical or emotional reactions while doing these exercises: your eyes and nose may water, phlegm may come up from your chest, you may cough, your sinuses may feel aggravated, you may feel tightness in your neck and shoulders, your heart may beat rapidly or feel painful, your body may twitch, you may even feel dizzy or nauseous. Buried memories may come flooding into your consciousness.

These symptoms are signs that the toning is working for you. It is stirring up emotional and physical blockages that have been preventing you from breathing normally and from living freely and openly. If you are accustomed to holding in your feelings, you may be afraid that something terrible is going to happen if you lose control. Releasing control for a while can lead to becoming relaxed and healthy. Having too much control leads to illness, including heart attacks and high blood pressure.

Some people are afraid that once they open up, they'll become violent or go crazy. I can assure you that I've never met anyone who became mentally or physically ill as a result of *expressing* their emotions. However, I have met innumerable people who became both mentally and physically ill as a result of *suppressing* their emotions.

Still, there is a fear—no matter how irrational—that once you open the box of repressed emotions and begin to let them out, you'll never get it closed again. After over twenty years of helping people with emotional release, the only problem I've seen occurs when people begin releasing their emotions and then get scared and try to close up the box.

Toning is one of the most powerful tools for releasing pent-up, repressed emotions. While doing these exercises, you may find yourself overcome by waves of deep feelings. There is no harm in this. In fact, it is the key to emotional and physical health. But if you are unaccustomed to releasing emotions, and if it is intensely disturbing to you, you may want to have someone present who you feel comfortable with, someone who will not be too upset by your emotions, and perhaps someone who can hold and comfort you if the need arises.

If you know that you have a lot of pain to release, and you're not sure that you can handle it—alone or with a friend—seek the help of a trained counselor or therapist and ask this person to work with you as you use these exercises.

There are other precautions that you can take. Before you begin working, sit quietly and take ten deep breaths. Tell yourself, "I give myself permission to temporarily lose control. I will not do harm to myself or to anyone else." Repeat this three times. This is like making a pact or an agreement with your subconscious mind. I've never seen anyone violate such an agreement once it was made.

If you feel upset during or after doing these exercises, just sit quietly again and bring ten deep breaths all the way down to your abdomen. You should be able to see your abdomen expand each time you inhale. This will help to calm and ground you. People usually feel considerably lighter and better after doing these exercises. They breathe better, their sinuses open and they feel empowered. Most people delight in discovering that they enjoy making sounds as their voices become stronger, fuller and more vibrant.

If you would like to do the exercises described in this book, but find that you just can't do them—if you can't even begin to open your mouth and make loud sounds—you were probably punished for being noisy when you were a child. Punishment can take the form of a harsh look or a strap. Very sensitive children respond to a sharp glance as if they'd been hit.

Even if you weren't punished, you may have internalized the idea that it is "bad," "naughty," "inconsiderate" and "obnoxious" to make loud noises. For a child, it is a matter of survival to be accepted by your caregivers, so most children learn to behave in a way that is acceptable to the adults. Even after we are grown up, when we behave in ways that our care-givers did not approve of, it triggers that old fear of abandonment. So when someone asks you to make loud noises, even if you think it's a good idea, you may find that you simply can't do it.

One way to overcome this resistance is to start by humming. Follow the exercises and hum instead of toning or groaning or making loud noises. When you get comfortable with humming, make a louder hum. As you notice that nothing terrible happens, you'll be able to let yourself make louder noises.

The important thing is to *release* any pent-up feelings that you may have, to *express* your emotions and feel your feelings. As you're doing this, you may find yourself yawning, screaming, crying. Your body may jerk, shiver or tremble. You may find that you want to pound on the bed with your fists or stomp your feet. If you are standing, you may want to fall down on the mat.

Just let it happen. If your body is twitching and jerking, this is a good sign. It means that your body is finally breaking free of its armoring, and you will probably feel much better after you finish the exercise. Give yourself as much acceptance as you possibly can, and let yourself release whatever needs releasing. Exaggerate your sounds. If you notice that your voice is beginning to sound like a siren, then make a loud siren noise. If you're starting to sound like a dog howling, then *become* a howling dog. If you sound like a baby crying, then become a baby calling out desperately for its mama. Don't worry about sounding silly. Try not to make judgments on yourself.

Welcome the emotions, no matter how painful or how wonderful. Emotions that are pent up are in some sense limiting or poisoning you, causing your breath to be short, hardening your heart, and suppressing the free flow of your energy.

Instead of shying away from the exercise because it seems to be making things worse, try going more deeply into it; instead of doing it for five minutes, try it for ten. You may get worse before you get better, but this is almost certainly going to help you. By the end of the session, you are likely to notice a distinct change for the better.

Exercise: Discovering and Releasing Your Voice

This exercise can be done with a poem, a song, an affirmation, or whatever you choose to use. The following poem was written by Chava

Lasson, and it is effective for bringing up emotions connected with suppressing the voice in childhood.

For example, Sylvia was a teacher who seemed self-confident, but she was extremely soft-spoken, and people often had to ask her to repeat what she said. She had a pleasant singing and toning voice, but it didn't have much resonance or power to it.

Sylvia read the following poem repeatedly, and every few lines she would stop, choked up with emotion, as the memories came flooding in. She grew up in a family where her mother and older brother spent hours at the piano, singing together. Sylvia was told that she did not have a very good voice, so she decided at an early age that she would not compete with these prima donnas. She became very quiet and excelled at writing instead of at singing.

But secretly, she loved to sing. It made her feel overwhelmingly sad that she never had the opportunity to express herself in this way. As she did this exercise, she got in touch with a massive inferiority complex that she had successfully hidden from herself and from others. She realized how much she had been denying herself, how much she had been holding back from the full realization of her potential. Each time she got in touch with a way in which she had held back her voice, she understood how she had been limiting her own power. As her voice grew stronger and more vibrant, her self-confidence grew with it.

After doing this exercise, Sylvia found that suddenly she was not afraid; her voice projected with calm self-assurance. She felt good about herself; she didn't have to apologize for her existence. Later, she found that she no longer felt frightened when she had to talk to a telephone operator or a teller at the bank. By empowering her voice, she empowered herself.

———————

1) Read the following aloud.

2) Read it again, in a loud voice, slowly and deliberately enunciating each syllable. Do not attempt to give emotional impact with this reading.

3) Sing it. Don't worry, this isn't a performance; just do the best you can.

4) Sing it again, with feeling.

5) Finally, read it again.

You will probably notice that the second reading is more powerful and expressive than the first.

> Give me the voice
> Give me the voice
> Give me the voice
> To say Thank-you
> For all you have given
> And all you have taken away
> Give me the voice
> To rejoice
> In your never-ending splendors
> From your minutest cells
> To your exploding galaxies
> Give me the voice of silence
> Yet penetrating the heavens
> To proclaim your eternal presence

Thanks to Chava Lasson for this poem and the exercise.

Exercise: Groaning and Moaning

This is a short emotional release exercise that you can do while you're in the shower, or driving on a back country road. It is an excellent way to start the day, or to wind down after work or after an argument or any stressful encounter. It gives you an opportunity to express your feelings and exaggerate everything you feel by dramatizing it with sound.

Scrunch up your mouth and eyes and make ugly, disgusting faces. Give yourself permission to be gross. Begin making low, groaning, moaning sounds. Let go and feel sorry for yourself. Make loud, complaining, ugly, disgusting sounds. Let your voice dredge up all the frustration, annoyance and grief that you feel about anyone and anything.

Eventually your voice will go up into the high register and down again. As you release tension and begin to feel better, your voice will probably go higher for longer. At some point, you'll feel a definite release and a levelling off. You may sigh, or tone a long note. You will know when you are finished. This typically takes five to ten minutes, but it varies from person to person (the first time may be much longer), so just continue until you feel complete.

Exercise: Giving Voice to the Emotions

This is a longer exercise that will help you dredge up and release buried emotions. Here is one possible scenario, but feel free to invent your own.

Walk up and down the room. Feel your emotions rising in your heart or wherever they feel strongest. Allow your body to express your feelings by the way you walk. (Head downcast or thrust upward; chest collapsed or pushed forward; steps small and fearful or long and forceful.)

Imagine that you're a character in a dramatic play or opera. Get into the feelings of your character. Feel the depth of emotions surge through you. Feel the intensity of your grief, anger or exultation. Remember that the success of your performance is going to depend upon your ability to convey your feelings through your voice.

Open your mouth and bring your feelings up from your heart (or wherever you feel them) and out of your mouth. Belt it out. Sing from the depths of your emotion.

You may want to sing a familiar song with deep soulful intonation, or you may just make sound without meaning, as if you were singing an opera in an unknown foreign tongue. The important thing is the drama. Express as much feeling as you possibly can.

To illustrate how this might work, let me give an example of how one woman used this exercise: Lorna had been waiting four months for her lover to return from Europe. He hadn't written or called for weeks, and she felt like she was going crazy from worry, insecurity and anxiety.

When given this exercise, she paced up and down the room, forcefully grabbing hairpins out of her hair, throwing them onto the floor, breathing heavily as her long abundant brown hair tumbled down over her shoulders. She looked like the formidable Brunnhilda in the Wagnerian opera as she belted out her powerful voice. Though she used no coherant words, there was no doubt that she was attacking him for having been treacherous, telling him that he had been treating her abominably, and she was determined to let the gods hear about it!

After this magnificent display, Lorna fell onto the couch utterly spent, tears and black mascara running together in dark valleys upon her cheeks. I urged her to continue breathing deeply.

Within a few minutes, she sat bolt-upright and gave me a radiant smile. "I feel *great!*" she announced. "I got my power back!" She was ecstatic. "I don't *need* him anymore. I'm my own woman!"

Lorna's boyfriend never did come back. She used toning many times to help her mourn his loss and to rebuild her self-esteem.

Exercise: Movement and Toning

Toning is even more effective when combined with movement. This exercise is great for dancers and people who like to express themselves with their bodies.

Stand up and give yourself plenty of space to move around.

Scan through your body (as described under *Toning for the Pain in Your Body*) and find out where you are holding your feelings.

Allow yourself to experience your feelings at a gut level. (The "gut" is usually felt below the navel, but some people report "gut feelings" from the stomach, above the navel.) When you get in touch with these feelings, let them rise up from your intestines to your stomach, and up your esophagus (food pipe), into your mouth. Now *taste* your mouth. What is the sensation in your mouth? Is it dry, moist, rough, smooth, slippery, sand-papery, sour, sweet, bitter, vomitty, stale? Where do you feel the most activity? Is it in your throat, your jaw, your teeth, your gums, or the tip of your tongue?

Feel the emotional connection between the taste or texture in your mouth and the place where you are holding your feelings. Allow the visceral feeling to form a shape in your mouth. Allow your body to express this taste, this shape, this visceral feeling. Begin by moving your hands, your arms, your head and neck.

While you are moving your body, as you taste this sensation, find the sound resonance of it. Allow your voice to express the taste and the feeling. Open your mouth and let out your voice. You may moan or scream or hiss. Your mouth may take on strange shapes and your voice will follow the shape of your mouth.

Allow your entire body to move as you let yourself express the feeling, the taste and the sound that you are experiencing. As you move, the taste will change, and as it changes, express that change with your movements and your sound.

Stay with the expression and release until you feel satisfied. This may take a few minutes, or it may take hours. This is an exercise that can be done individually, or in a group.

When Sarah did this exercise, she was feeling depressed and weak. She started out with a low hum. As she warmed to the process, she moved her arms in and out, leading with the elbows, like a cormorant drying her wings. She pursed her lips, making a high sound, repeating that sound again and again until it began to vibrate and then it moved into a fearful sound as she tilted back her chin and began to crow like a great prehistoric bird sounding a warning. Then she stomped around the room, using a low deep aggressive sound, as though she were protecting her kill.

When she finished, she said she had no intellectual understanding of what had happened, but she did experience a release in her body, and she felt much more energetic and enthusiatic.

Thanks to Ruth Gould Goodman for this exercise.

10

THE CHAKRAS AND VIBRATIONAL HEALING

The essence of holistic healing is that each person is more than the sum of his or her parts. The old medical model sees the body as a machine, and the doctor as a body mechanic. Many people still believe that we are merely physical beings with moving parts, and that the parts eventually break down or wear out and need to be repaired. It is a relatively new concept in western medicine that the mind, emotions and spirit have a profound effect upon health maintenance, susceptibility to disease and the ability to heal.

The chakras

Things have changed somewhat since 1974 when Dr. Hans Selye demonstrated that mental and emotional stress have a definite predictable effect on the physical body.[1] From 1974 to 1981 Dr. O. Carl Simonton and Stephanie Matthews Simonton conducted a study which demonstrated that cancer patients (they were working with advanced lung, bowel and breast cancer) lived about twice as long when they had a higher motivation to live, as enhanced by visualization, meditation and other methods which they described in their book, *Getting Well Again*. In 1989, similar results were published by researchers at Stanford University and The University of California at Berkeley.[2]

Though most physicians have not yet accepted her work, Louise Hay identifies an underlying emotional or spiritual cause for every physical ailment,[3] and many AIDS patients are being helped by her insights. [4]

The fact that the mind, emotions and spirit interact with the physical body has been known to practitioners of Ayurvedic and traditional Chinese Medicine for thousands of years. Shamanic Doctors and Hawaiian Kahunas have used ritual, song, dance, herbs and crystals to heal body, mind, emotions and spirit since time immemorial.

Chakra is a Sanskrit word that means wheel or vortex. A chakra is an invisible (to the normal human eye) center of spinning energy. There are seven chakras which are located at points along the spine. The chakra system is part of an ancient Ayurvedic Hindu tradition that recognizes the influence of subtle forces on the human body. It is believed that energies enter the physical body from the invisible auric body by way of these chakras. For holistic practitioners, the chakra system is the ideal tool for coordinating the treatment of body, mind, emotions and spirit.

There is no better exercise than *Toning the Chakras* if you want to "tune up" your body, mind, emotions and spirit with your own voice. You can tone without any knowledge of the chakras, but understanding the chakra system gives another dimension to the experience of toning. In order to develop this understanding, the exercises in this chapter will cover 1) the locations, colors, internal organs and energies of the chakras, 2) color breathing to charge the chakras, and 3) how to combine color breathing with toning.

The chakras can be visualized along the spine from the front of the body, or from the back. Through inner vision, some people can see the energies and colors emanating from the chakras. Others can feel this energy by holding the open hand, palm down, a couple of inches above the body at the area of the chakra, and moving the hand in a clockwise or counter-clockwise direction.

This movement allows the energy emanating from the hand to get caught up in the energy vibrating from the chakra and it is possible to feel the shape, intensity and temperature of the spin of energy from the chakra. The experience is similar to dipping your hand in the ocean to feel the temperature of the water and the pull of the current. By feeling the spin, one can determine whether the chakra is relatively open or closed. Another way of detecting the balance of the chakras is simply by understanding their properties, and analyzing a person on that basis.

It is not within the scope of this book to go into great detail about the chakras. If you would like to learn more about this system, please see my book, *Color and Crystals, A Journey Through the Chakras* (Crossing Press). Here is a brief description of the seven chakras:

The first chakra is located at the tailbone and it includes the bladder, large intestines, penis, scrotum and vagina. The color is red. It relates to the material plane and the physical body. The energy of the first chakra tends to be strong if you received unconditional love and affection as a child. Then you will probably feel good about yourself and your body, which will influence your ability to manifest what you desire in the material world. The first chakra affects your blood flow, nervous system and vitality. If you did not receive unconditional love and affection as a child, your first chakra energy may be weak, and it may respond to the color red and the tone E as in "red."

The second chakra is located below between the navel and the pubic bone. It includes the kidneys, uterus, fallopian tubes and ovaries. The color is orange. This is the center of sexuality, sociability and friendliness. The energy here reflects how you feel about your sexuality, which tends to be influenced by how your parents felt about sexuality, how your peers felt about sexuality during your formative years, and your own early sexual experiences. This is also the center of the emotions—particularly emotions that relate to sexuality. It governs gut-level intuition. It is also the center of desire—not just for sex, but for anything that you want. If you are afraid of people and of sexuality, then your second chakra may be weak, and it may respond to the color orange and the tone O as in "home."

The third chakra is located above the navel (between the navel and the breast bone) and below the diaphragm, at the solar plexus. It includes the small intestines, liver, spleen, adrenal glands and diaphragm. The color is yellow. This is the center of your personal power—your gift. The energy

[handwritten margin notes: RED, with phonetic markings E, E, [E]; O; [O]]

here will reflect whether you have discovered and given expression to the part of you that is unique and special. Your sense of self-worth and self-esteem will be reflected in the energy of the third chakra. It is also an emotional center and one of the centers of intelligence. Yellow is an expansive color, so it is the color of relaxation. Almost all the organs of digestion are located here, so this is the chakra that governs digestion. If you have low self-esteem, your third chakra energy may be weak and it may respond to the color yellow and the tone AOM.

The fourth chakra is located at the chest. It includes the heart, lungs and thymus gland. This is the central chakra, with three above and three below. There are two colors that relate to the heart chakra: pink and green. This is the center of unconditional love and compassion, through which we feel a sense of identification with other people, plants, animals and all of life. This is our most vulnerable chakra, because when we're hurt in love, the first impulse is to close our hearts and say, "I'll never let anyone do that to me again." The challenge is to feel our feelings and allow our hearts to be open. Since it is located in the middle of all the chakras, this is where we bring together the emotions, mind and spirit. If you have built a wall around your heart, your fourth chakra energy may be weak and it may respond to pink or green and to the tone AH as in "hah."

The fifth chakra is located at the base of the throat. It includes the throat, thyroid and parathyroid glands. The color is blue. The throat chakra is the center of communication. It also relates to opening the door to spirituality. This is the first of the top three chakras, which are all considered spiritual centers. Toning helps to open all of the chakras, but it has the strongest effect on the throat chakra, since this is the home of the vocal cords and the voice box (larynx). If you have difficulty with communication and you feel shy about singing or toning, your fifth chakra energy is probably weak and it may respond to the color blue and to the tone UU as in "blue."

The sixth chakra is located between the eyebrows at the third eye. It includes the brain and pituitary gland. The color is indigo (a purplish blue). Clear-minded intelligence and inner vision are associated with the third eye. This is the chakra that allows you to experience telepathy, astral travel and past lives. It is the center of higher knowledge that enables you to have an intuitive grasp of various aspects of metaphysics such as astrology and the Tarot. When this center is open and balanced, you will experience a feeling of open-mindedness tempered with a moderate amount of healthy skepticism. When this chakra is closed, there is superstitious fear—usually due to early religious training—about metaphysical topics. When this chakra is weak, it may respond to indigo and the tone M as in "mom."

The seventh chakra is located at the top of the head and it includes the brain and the pineal gland. The color is violet. This is where the baby's soft spot, the fontanelle, is located. The Hopi call this the "window of the soul," and many mystics believe that this is where the soul enters and exits the human body. Through the crown chakra we experience Enlightenment and Divine Bliss—a sense of perfect union with Spirit. If you feel no connection with Spirit, then this chakra is probably weak and it may respond to violet and the tone EE as in "glee."

Each chakra has a distinct color, and there are different schools of thought about which colors characterize which chakra. The method I use follows the rainbow.

Vibrational Healing is the use of various vibrational tools such as sound, crystals, color and aromatherapy in conjunction with other healing modalities. Over the past twenty years, I have developed a unique form of Vibrational Healing that I call *Vibrational Alignment,* which combines Vibrational Healing with intuitive counseling and a broad range of transpersonal healing modalities, bringing the energy of the chakras into balance and the body into harmonious alignment with the earth and heavens. To give you a better idea of how the chakras are used for healing, and so that you may see how toning can be used in conjunction with other healing modalities, I will describe a *Vibrational Alignment.*

The chakras are a perfect system through which to comprehend the universe and the individual. When the energy of all the chakras is in balance, then a person will experience health and harmony in body, mind, emotions and spirit. Through the technique of *Vibrational Alignment,* I can "feel" the degree to which each chakra is open or closed.

People have different psychic skills: one person sees auras, another person hears voices, and yet another person feels energies. Feeling the energy of the chakras is one of my gifts, and most of my students have learned to do this without difficulty. However, some students prefer to use a pendulum.

Since we are all basically vibratory packages of energy, illness can be seen as a disruption or an imbalance in that energy. So while I do not set out to heal specific illnesses, many people find that their ailments simply disappear after receiving a *Vibrational Alignment.*

The method I use to achieve this realignment is a combination of in-depth counseling combined with the use of tools that vibrate with considerable intensity: sound (toning), light (color), crystals and aromas. Through the perfection of their innate being, the flowers and crystals share their energetic resonance with us, and by being in their presence, we remember our own perfection. When the practitioner is reasonably aligned at all of her/his own chakras, and when the intuitive faculties are therefore in good alignment, the healer can readily perceive which colors and tones are required to bring the chakras into alignment.

The training to become a practitioner of this art is expressed in the idea, "Physician, Heal Thyself." You simply cannot do this work until your own chakras are cleansed, balanced and aligned, so the training to become a Vibrational Healer is truly a journey of the soul.

You can never heal another human being unless they are ready to heal themselves. Every illness is a gift—an opportunity for growth, cleansing and renewal. If we simply take away the illness, then we have deprived a person of his or her gift. So as true healers, our function is to work with people to help them to grasp the nature of the challenge that their illness, or discomfort, or grief has brought to them.

If it is a grief—a blockage of the heart—then we provide an opportunity for the person to release their pain and drain their pool of sorrow so they can go into the future without having to carry so great a weight. Often it is the role of the healer to simply listen, and allow their clients to heal themselves. This is not an easy role for one who is eager to play an active role, to be the center of attention, or to be an authority figure.

I think of the Vibrational Healer as being more like a midwife: facilitating, sharing tools, providing a safe place to get in touch with and release pent-up feelings, giving unconditional love and support to clients so that they can do whatever they need to do for themselves. I think the long hugs that we exchange after each session are an essential part of the healing process.

When I do a *Vibrational Alignment*, I use my toning crystal—as explained in this chapter under *Toning with Crystals*—to "feel" the spin of energy at the feet, knees, hips, and each of the chakras. This can be done simply with the hand, or with a pendulum. Each chakra or part of the body relates to a specific aspect of a person's whole being. For example, the energy at the feet tells whether a person is on his or her Life Path—is this person going forward in life or is he/she holding back? The energy at the first chakra tells whether a person received unconditional love and affection as a child. The energy at the fourth chakra tells whether this person has built walls around his or her heart.

The normal span of energy at the chakras is about equivalent to the circumference of a person's open hand. The normal shape of the spin is a simple circle. The normal rate of spin is comparable to the pulse of the heart; a cycle is completed with each "lub-dub" of the heartbeat. Any significant variation on these norms indicates an imbalance of the chakras. A rapid rate of spin, for example, could indicate excessive energy at the chakra. An elliptical spin could indicate deficiency in some area relevant to that chakra.

For example, the energy at the feet tells me whether that person is on their path in life. Just by feeling the spin of energy at the feet, I can tell— with amazing accuracy—whether that person is focused about their life path. I can feel if that person is "walking in their own shoes" (the energy feels strong and makes a full circle from the tip of the toes down to the heel) or whether they are "walking on eggshells" or "tiptoeing around other people" (the energy feels weak and the circle centers around the ball of the foot and doesn't reach down as far as the heel). By feeling the spin of energy at each part of the body, I can discover imbalances that a person may not even be aware of.

When the spin is out of balance, I work with a client until the energy comes into balance. I do this through a combination of speaking about issues related to this chakra, using light hypnosis to guide the person through childhood traumas, or through their birth, or their conception, or their past lives, or between lives.

While doing this, I place appropriate crystals on their body, I make tones to free up, strengthen or remove energies, and I may use essential oils at areas of the body corresponding with the chakras. I do not expect the crystals or tones to heal in and of themselves (though sometimes they do); I see them as fellow-healers, with all of us working together to create harmony and balance in the universe and within this individual.

Let's look at an example. Lana was having trouble with severe head-aches, and she wanted help in finding her Life Path. When I felt the energy at her feet—especially at her right foot, which is the male side (the right side of the body relates to men and to the father; the left side relates to women and to the mother)— the spin would go half way around, and then stop. Then it would start up, go half way around, slow down and stop again. I deduced from this that she was holding herself back in some way, which would become clear as I was working on the chakras.

The chakras were reasonably well balanced until I came to her third eye, which indicates whether a person is open to spiritual, psychic and metaphysical areas. Here the energy moved in an elliptical pattern rather than a circle. This indicates that a person is open in most respects, but narrowed down in others.

I knew that Lana did Tarot readings, so I was surprised to find that she was partly shut off at her third eye. When I inquired about her early religious training—which is the usual source of constriction at the sixth chakra—she began talking about her uncle, a trance channel, who had been severely ridiculed by their family when Lana was a child. Consequently, Lana admitted that she felt distrustful about anything that involved channeling.

You might wonder why it should matter whether Lana had a resistance to channeling; after all, some people believe in such things and some don't. I have found that any place where the energy is blocked prevents a free flow of energy through that part of the body, which impedes the flow of energy throughout the entire physical and auric bodies, leading to emotional and/ or physical imbalance.

It was time to balance the energies. I asked her to think of an odor that reminded her of her childhood, and she chose ginger and cinnamon. I put a little vegetable oil at her third eye and rubbed in a bit of powdered ginger and cinnamon. Then I placed a purple and black sugilite at her third eye, because this stone is comforting to psychically sensitive children (who are often painfully sensitive to teasing). At her throat I placed a stone of azurite and malachite combined; malachite helps bring up repressed feelings and azurite stimulates the throat chakra, encouraging a person to talk about those feelings.

Then I toned spontaneously, and I noticed that the tones that came out of my mouth had a sad, mournful quality to them. I used light hypnosis and regressed her into her childhood. She clearly remembered her uncle being teased and humiliated, and she relived an incident in which she was one of the children who actually threw rocks at him. She had repressed this memory, and tears came to her eyes as she recalled the incident. I asked if she wanted to make a sound to express her feelings and though she had never toned before, she instantly went into a high wail, keening and crying for several minutes. When her grief was spent, I asked if she could forgive herself. As she thought about this, I toned the soothing UU sound of the throat chakra (which helps open to spirituality), mentally directing blue light to her head and heart.

When she said, "Yes, I do think I can forgive myself," I asked if she could visualize being with her uncle as a grown woman. When she did this,

I asked if she wanted to apologize to him. As she did, I toned the MM sound of the third eye chakra.

I asked if she wanted to ask him to pass his gift on to her, and she was amazed to realize that this was truly her heart's desire. I put an in-and-out crystal at her third eye (as explained in my book, *Color and Crystals*) which would help bring out her hidden talents as I toned the MM sound again. She was quiet for a long time. (I honor people's silence. Often this is the fullest experience for them—a time when they are processing more than they could possibly express.) At some point during this silence, I had a sudden urge to make a loud, dramatic, high-pitched sound. I did this, and then lapsed into silence again.

Finally she spoke. She told me how fond she had been of her uncle, and how people said she took after him. When he became a trance channel, her parents turned against him. Her mother (his sister) spoke of him as if he were the Devil, and it frightened young Lana.

As she relived this incident, Lana realized that she had projected all her fears about herself onto her uncle. It pained her deeply to reject and hurt him. She marvelled that the dramatic, high-pitched tone that I made during her silence occurred at exactly the moment of her realization, and the sound seemed to literally break through and shatter her old fears.

I guided her to go to her uncle in her mind's eye and embrace this beloved man while I toned AH for her heart and sent pink light to both of them. She felt an incredible flood of energy coursing through her heart and all the way up to her crown chakra.

When I removed the crystals and felt her sixth chakra again, the spin was healthy and the circle was full. A couple months later I ran into her and she told me that she had begun channeling.

Now we can proceed to the exercises that relate to the chakras.

Exercise: Color Breathing

Color is one of the vibratory tools that can be used to heal body, mind, emotions and spirit. One way of using color for healing is by charging each chakra with its corresponding color. This can be done through visualizing the color while performing this breathing technique. Later, we will combine color breathing with toning for maximum effectiveness.

Look out at a green meadow (or imagine that you are doing so) and take in a long, deep breath, as if you were pulling the green of the grass directly into your lungs. When you do this, you are charging your heart chakra with green light.

The colors of the first three chakras (red, orange and yellow) are associated with the earth. Visualize these colors arcing up from the earth like a rainbow, and entering each of the corresponding chakras. The heart chakra has two colors: pink and green. Visualize one or both colors coming directly across the horizon, toward your heart. The colors of the top three chakras (blue, indigo and violet) are associated with the heavens. Think of each of these colors arcing down from the sky like inverted rainbows, entering each corresponding chakra (see illus. pg. 123).

In the following exercise, I've given the colors of the rainbow, but you can use any color at any part of the body. Experiment to see what works best for you. Any color may be used at any chakra, so it is impossible to make a mistake. However, certain colors can make you feel very uncomfortable when used in excess (especially red, and—to a lesser extent—blue). Pay close attention to your feelings while working with the colors, and if you begin to feel physically or emotionally uncomfortable, discontinue that color. If the color makes you feel particularly good, you may want to continue using it for ten or twenty breaths. For more information about how to work with colors, see my book, *Color and Crystals, A Journey Through the Chakras*.

Take ten deep breaths. Feel your abdomen expanding. Each time you exhale, feel your abdomen gently contracting and release all tension and negativity.

Focus on your *first chakra* at your tailbone. The color is red. Visualize this color arcing up from the earth. Inhale and draw red into your first chakra. Exhale and fix it there. Repeat three times. Notice how this feels. (People tend to have a strong reaction to red. Some people feel warm and relaxed, while others feel highly stimulated, nervous, or even angry.)

Bring your attention to your *second chakra*, below your navel. The color is orange. See this color arcing up from the earth. Inhale and draw orange into your second chakra. Exhale and fix it there. Repeat three times. Notice how this feels.

Bring your attention to your *third chakra*, above your navel. The color is yellow. See this color arcing up from the earth. Inhale and draw yellow into your third chakra. Exhale and fix it there. Repeat three times. Notice how this feels.

Focus on your *fourth chakra*, at your chest. The color is green. See this color coming directly across the horizon. Inhale and bring

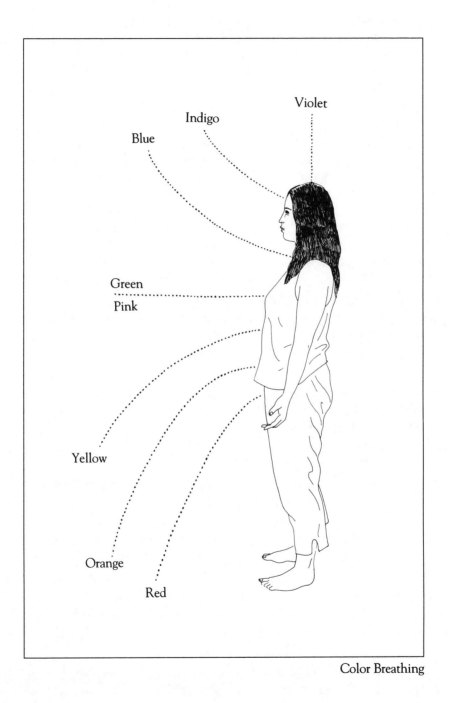

Color Breathing

this color into your heart chakra. Exhale and fix it there. Repeat three times. Notice how this feels. (Repeat the same instructions, using pink.)

Focus on your *fifth chakra*, at the base of your throat. The color is blue. See this color arcing *down* from the heavens. Inhale and bring this color into your throat. Exhale and fix it there. Repeat three times. Notice how this feels.

Focus on your *sixth chakra*, at your third eye. The color is indigo. See this color arcing down from the heavens. Inhale and bring this color into your third eye. Exhale and fix it there. Repeat three times. Notice how this feels.

Focus on your *seventh chakra*, at the crown of your head. The color is violet. See this color coming directly down from the heavens. Inhale and bring this color into the top of your head. Exhale and fix it there. Repeat three times. Notice how this feels.

In the foregoing exercise, you have been bringing colored light to yourself. Now you can practice sending color to another person. Always begin by filling *yourself* with color. You are not ready to help another peson until your own chakras are overflowing with color.

When you project color toward another person, your most powerful sending devices are 1) your solar plexus (third chakra), 2) your heart (fourth chakra) and 3) your third eye (sixth chakra). If you want to send color to another person, you can use your solar plexus to send red, orange and yellow; use your heart to send pink and green and use your third eye to send blue, indigo and violet.

For example, if your friend, Annette, is having problems with low self-esteem, you might want to help her strengthen her third chakra. First you would visualize the color yellow arcing up from the earth to your own third chakra as you inhale. Exhale and fix it there. Do this at least three times, or until you feel that you have plenty of yellow at your third chakra.

On your next inhale, draw in the colored light less deeply and then, as you exhale, visualize the yellow light looping around and radiating out through your solar plexus directly toward your friend's third chakra. To make this even more effective, ask her to inhale and visualize the yellow light coming into her third chakra as you exhale.

If your friend is having difficulty communicating, you could help her to strengthen her throat chakra. Begin by visualizing blue light arcing down from the heavens as you inhale, and fix it at your throat as you exhale. Do this at least three times, or until you feel that you have plenty of blue at your fifth chakra. On your next inhale, imagine it dipping into your throat chakra and then rising up directly through your neck and head to your third eye. On the exhale, beam it out through your third eye, like a laser, directly toward your friend's throat.

Color breathing (with or without toning) can be done in the presence of the person you are sending it to, or in his or her absence. The same technique can be used for distant healing, but instead of directing the color to a person who is directly in front of you, visualize the person in your mind and direct the color to that person *as if* he were standing in front of you.

Experiment with sending colors to friends over the phone, and in various situations, and ask for feedback about the results. Play around with combinations of colors and chakras. You don't need to limit color breathing to the chakras. For example, an infant was tagging along with his big brother until the big boy got impatient and "accidentally" stepped on the little one's toe. While holding and rocking the little one, his mother sent the pink light of love from her heart to his heart and then she sent cooling blue by way of her third eye to his toe. He stopped crying immediately, and was soon back on his feet, hurrying to catch up with his big brother.

Exercise: Toning the Chakras

You can derive great benefit from using your voice to vibrate and strengthen your own chakras. You can also tone for others, to energize their chakras. According to Dr. Alfred A. Tomatis, we charge the brain when we speak or sing, and the greatest charge is derived from the higher frequencies (which correlate with the higher notes—which correspond to the higher chakras). The most effective way to charge the brain and thus the body, is by using a rising curve in your sound. [5]

In this exercise, concentrate on making a single sound (such as AH) on a single note (such as f) that will stimulate the chakra (in this case, the heart chakra, which is the fourth) by bringing vibratory energy into it. This exercise takes you through the chakras in a rising progression of tones. If time permits, the tones for the higher chakras can be repeated more frequently than the tones for the lower chakras, to increase the charge to your brain. The tones are repeated several times on the rising curve, for the greatest stimulation. They are made only once for each chakra while descending, to help ground you without losing the high of your charge.

When learning to tone for a given chakra, place your fingertips lightly over that chakra. Begin by trying the tones that I recommend, then experiment with different tones on different notes until you find a sound that causes a vibration beneath your fingertips.

There are many systems of toning. For the sake of simplicity, I have given the c major scale as a guideline for moving through the chakras, beginning with middle c at the tailbone, and ending with b at the crown. Start out by using these notes and tones, but feel free to experiment. The main guideline is that the note for the second chakra should be higher than the note for the first chakra, and so on, with the note for the seventh being the highest. But the notes don't have to begin with c, and they don't have to progress just one note at a time.

In my practice, I do not use the scale of c major, and I probably use different notes at different times, but I do use low notes for the lower chakras and high notes for the higher chakras. When I am healing with my voice, I do not pay attention to specific notes; I just use the sounds that I feel intuitively moved to use.

The most important factor in toning for the chakras is to make a tone (the combination of a sound and a note) that—for you—vibrates the chakras. There is no right or wrong, and you don't have to be musically inclined to be good at toning. People who have no ear for music can have wonderful results.

As you do this exercise, you will be combining toning with color breathing, as learned in the previous exercise. The following chart gives the color, note and tone for each chakra, and an "as in" word to clarify how the tone should sound (example: E *as in* red).

Chakra	Color	Note	Tone	As In
First	red	c	E	r<u>e</u>d
Second	orange	d	O	h<u>o</u>me
Third	yellow	e	AOM	<u>a</u>men & h<u>o</u>me & m<u>o</u>m
Fourth	green & pink	f	AH	h<u>ah</u>
Fifth	blue	g	UU	bl<u>u</u>e
Sixth	indigo	a	MM	mo<u>m</u>
Seventh	violet	b	EE	gl<u>ee</u>

Proceed exactly as you did in the *Color Breathing Exercise,* but every time you inhale a color, your exhale will be accompanied by the tone that corresponds to that chakra.

Begin by playing each of the notes on a piano or tuning fork. Begin with middle c and as you play the note, breathe in the color red and as you exhale, make the tone E, as in "red." Tone at least three times at each energy center, so you have the oppportunity to experience the sound and to feel the beneficial effects of the tones and colors.

Each chakra has just one sound, with the exception of the third chakra, which is the center of personal power. When you are truly in your power, you are open at all the chakras. Thus you can tap into your center of power at the heart (AH) and your center of power at the second chakra (O), which is in the middle of the three lower chakras, and your center of power at the third eye or sixth chakra (MM) which is in the middle of the three higher chakras.

The combined tones of AOM create a clear expression of completely balanced personal power. Doing all three tones con-secutively on the same musical note centers you at the third chakra.

Continue to make one sound for each chakra, as shown on the chart, and repeat each tone three or more times until you reach the crown chakra.

Once you reach the crown chakra, you may feel quite blissful, and you may want to go into meditation, sitting quietly and breathing deeply for at least five minutes. When you feel ready to return to your body, toning provides a simple method for getting grounded after dipping into the bliss of higher consciousness.

Come down the same way that you went up—but in reverse. Tone once for the crown chakra while visualizing the color violet, then tone once for the third eye while visualizing the color indigo, and so forth until you come back to the first chakra. Tone just once at each chakra. This inverse process brings you progressively closer and closer to the earth, and this in turn brings you into your body and your physical waking awareness so that by the time you come back to the first chakra, you are fully refreshed, grounded, and ready to function.

This is the exercise that is on my tape, *The Healing Voice—Toning Meditations* (see last page of this book).

Exercise: Souding Your Own Chakras

Now that you have thoroughly explored your chakras, you are ready for this exercise. Lie down on your back on a bed, or on a mat on the floor. You should have padding under your whole body and under your arms, without any pillows or anything in the way, because you may want to use your whole body vigorously. Alternately, you may prefer to do this exercise standing up, which gives you plenty of opportunity to move your body.

Begin by breathing deeply. Inhale through your nose and feel your abdomen expanding as you bring in as much air as you can. Hold the air until you feel a little bit uncomfortable, and then blow out the air through slightly pursed lips. Inhale and repeat the same process. Do this ten times.

Focus your attention at your first chakra. Notice the color. If you can't see the color that's there, just visualize red at your first chakra. Pay attention to your body: How does it feel at your genital area? Do you feel tense, nervous? Is there any pain? Do you feel hot or cold? As you focus at this area, does it bring up any feelings for you? Concentrate on those feelings for a minute and then give them a sound that describes how you feel at your first chakra.

Repeat this exercise at each of your chakras. If you can't see the colors that are there, refer to the colors in the chart on the previous exercise, *Toning for the Chakras*. Make a sound for each chakra, and then repeat the sound several times, or until you feel finished.

Most people begin at the first chakra and go up to the crown, but you may want to move around. This exercise can be used for balancing and healing. For example, if you feel blocked at the first chakra, you may only be able to make a small sound there. But after you've made a stronger sound at your second chakra, you may be able to go back to your first and break through the block. Alternately, after you've made a sound for your heart chakra, you may want to come back to your first again, and make a sound that will be explosive.

Continue the exercise until you've made sounds for all your chakras.

The order you go in is not important. The important thing is to *release* any pent-up feelings that you may have, to *express* your emotions and feel your feelings. This is a very powerful exercise for self-healing.

Exercise: The Expanded A-O-M

A person who has a well-balanced personality functions effectively on a day-to-day level with all of his or her chakras open, balanced and alert. The Expanded A-O-M is an exercise that balances body, mind, emotions and spirit. I like to end my Color and Toning Meditation with this exercise.

There are two ways to tone AOM. First there is the sound that goes with the third chakra. Here we have three syllables that are sounded consecutively on the same note, as in the previous exercise. Practice doing the AOM on the note e.

With the Expanded A-O-M, each tone is done individually, on a separate note, according to the notes of the three different chakras. The voice goes from AH on the note of f (if you don't have an instrument, you can just tone in the mid range), to O on the note of d (in the low range) to MM on the note of a (in the high range).

Begin by doing each tone with one exhalation of the breath. Then do all three tones, with their varying pitches, on one exhalation. The sound is peculiar to the ear, but it has a powerful effect on the body and the total energy, because it brings the physical (lower chakra) energy into alignment with the spiritual (higher chakra) energy at the heart center. While toning the Expanded A-O-M, visualize the color gold.

This is an excellent way to conclude any group or individual meditation. It leaves you feeling grounded and sublime at the same time.

Exercise: Toning with Crystals

Toning can be enhanced by the use of certain crystals, and Crystal Healing can be enhanced by toning. Crystals are amplifiers, and they are one of the most reliable ways to hold a particular vibration or frequency, which is why they're used in radios. Industrial crystals are grown in laboratories and cut in specific shapes for particular purposes. Cut crystals and laboratory crystals can be used for toning, but I prefer natural crystals. In any case, the crystal should be long and thin. Randall and Vicki Baer write in *The Crystal Connection* that "the longer the body and the greater the clarity and mass, the greater the amplification. A longer body also allows for a higher degree of versatile energy input and modulation potential."[6]

Toning Crystals are long, narrow and clear. They're either single or double terminated; i.e. they may have a point at one end, or points at both the top and the bottom, but if there is more than one point at the same end, they are not likely to be effective. Toning Crystals are not necessary for toning, but they can intensify the length and breadth of your sound vibrations.

When selecting a crystal for toning, try toning with it to see if you can hold the tones for longer, and if the tones feel stronger and more vibrant. Not every long narrow crystal is effective for toning, and some are far more powerful than others (not necessarily the longest ones).

Hold the crystal in your right hand (the right side is considered masculine, aggressive, and we tend to give from the right). Cradle the base of it (the non-pointed end) in the palm of your hand, or hold it along the shaft. You can hold the crystal at the level of your heart, pointing away from you as you tone for another person. (See illus. pg. 131.)

Crystal Healing with Toning. If you use crystals for healing, toning can enhance virtually any placement of the stones. Please review the Guidelines for Practitioners in Chapter Eight and the Guidelines for Emotional Release in Chapter Nine before using the following method on another person.

This simple technique requires at least one single-terminated clear quartz crystal, about two inches long. You will also want a smoky quartz crystal (a brown quartz), about the same size. Smoky quartz has the ability to remove negative energy from the body and to send it into the earth when it is pointed toward the feet. You can do this layout for yourself, but I will describe it here as if you were working on a woman, whom we will call Janet.

Ask Janet to lie with her head to the North. If Janet has a pain at some part of her body, place a single-terminated (one-pointed) smoky quartz (preferably) or clear quartz crystal over the painful place, pointing toward her feet (to enable the negative energy to drain out, into the earth). (See illus. pg. 132.)

If you have a toning crystal, point it at the crystal on her body. Make a tone that feels appropriate to break up the pain or imbalance, or make the corresponding sound for the chakra that is closest to the painful area.

Example: Janet has a tension headache, and she just had a fight with her boss. It sounds like a power struggle, so you suspect that she's having problems with her third chakra—the center of personal power. Ask her how her digestion has been. If she's been suffering from diarrhea or stomach aches, then there is a disruption

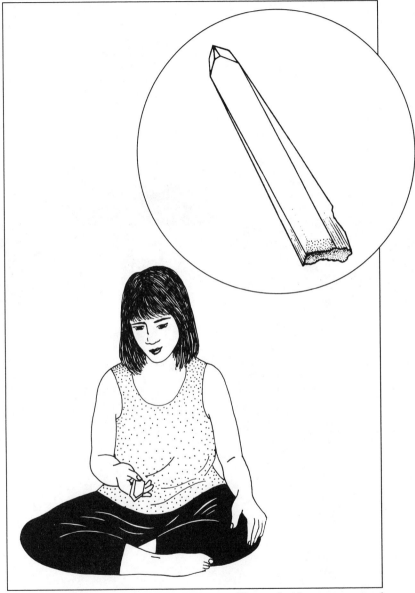

How to hold a toning crystal

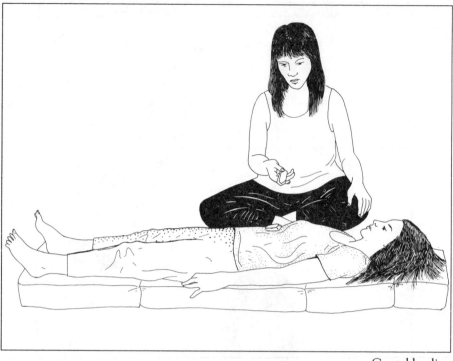

Crystal healing

of the third chakra energy. You can pull out negative energy by placing a smoky quartz crystal at her solar plexus, pointing toward her feet. Breathe in yellow light until your own third chakra feels full. Then inhale the yellow and on the exhale, send her yellow light while you tone AOM (or whatever sound feels appropriate) as you point your toning crystal toward the crystal on her solar plexus. Repeat three times and then ask if she wants more.

You can place several crystals on her body at the same time. Repeat this procedure for each one. If you suspect a weakness at the fifth chakra, for example, you can charge the chakra energetically by placing a clear quartz crystal at the throat, with the termination toward her head and then do the color breathing and toning as before, this time using blue light.

Cleansing the Stones: After using your crystals for healing purposes, be sure to cleanse them by holding them under cold running tap water, with the termination pointing toward the drain, for ten to twenty seconds or more. Since energy follows water, the undesireable energy will wash down the drain. You may also want to put your hands and wrists under cold running water.

11

TONING FOR PURE PLEASURE

Toning for pleasure is about being spontaneous and light-hearted, without any particular logic. So this will be a whimsical chapter, flitting about from one thing to another.

I returned recently to a commune in Northern California in the Siskiyou forest, where I lived twenty years ago, with eighty people on 200 acres of land. The commune is still there, with a few young people sharing the big house, communal garden and kitchen. They welcomed us (my husband, Gordon, my grown son, Reuben, and myself) and invited us to eat with them.

The next morning I awoke early and found Katya working in the garden. I helped her prepare a bed for the corn and beans, and we talked as we worked. She told me that she wanted to bring more spirituality into the life of the community, so we talked about meditating in the mornings and evenings, and holding hands before meals. Then she said that she and Tom, the main gardener, both enjoyed chanting.

Around this time, Tom joined us and I told them about the Hawaiian farmers who started each day by chanting and doing the hula. In the evening, before going home, they would do another chant and hula. All through the day, their work in the gardens was accompanied by chanted prayers.[1]

Tom brought out the corn and bean seeds. We made furrows, and started planting the beans. We talked about how, for the black slaves, motion and song went hand-in-hand. The cotton pickers began the day with song, they sang again when the sun set and when it was time to weigh in the cotton. Throughout the day, laborers sang while they worked. The rhythm of the work gave birth to song, and the singing gave energy to their work.[2]

Inspired by my own stories, I offered to teach them how to tone for the chakras (see Chapter Ten). They were pleased by the idea, so as we planted corn, we toned E as in "red" for the first chakra, repeating it several times, blending our voices until the sound was pleasant. Then we did O as in "home" for the second chakra. When we came to the third, which relates to the color yellow, we all noticed that the AOM sound felt especially good. When we did the AH sound at the heart, which relates to the color green, it sounded even better—as if it resonated in perfect harmony with the corn. We tried all the other chakras, but were unanimous in wanting to return to the heart chakra, feeling the AH sound to be the ideal accompaniment to planting corn.

We spent the next couple hours sharing chants while we gardened, spiritualizing and energizing our work and probably making those seeds very happy.

———

In the mid seventies, I had the opportunity to spend a weekend with an encampment of contemporary Hasidic Jews, with Rabbi Reb Zahlman, in Deadwood, Oregon. One of the things I loved the most was walking through the woods and hearing people singing constantly. They were singing while they were setting up camp, and while they were washing the dishes, and while they were walking down the path. I asked my Hasidic friend, Yehuda Landsman what was happening. This was his reply:

One of the real focuses in Hasidism is the idea of serving God with joy: in Hebrew it's *ha shem be simcha*—which comes right out of Psalms, which is basically King David's poetry, and it's really exquisite singing. As I recall, King David used to play a harp, or a lyre, and he sang those songs.

Hasidim really try to live by that idea, so there's this constant sense of singing, doing everything with song, just to be constantly in touch with the Divine. There's a sense of having a constant connection with the Divine from that place of joy.

I can tell you how it works for me. I'll oftentimes find myself sitting on the bus or walking down the street, and I'll start singing *nigun*, that wordless kind of melody. And I'll just bury myself into the melody and take myself into an altered state of consciousness through that. It's just a way of saying, "Okay. I'm living here in the world, and I am of the world, but I don't want to lose that connection to my higher self."

An interesting thing happened, actually, on Friday. I was standing waiting for the telephone down in Oakland, and I got lost in a melody. And someone I knew came up—she must have said hello to me two or three times—and she said, "Boy, you were really in another world!"

I was just singing real quietly to myself. For me, at least, I have to actually voice the song, but it can be really quiet, so just I can hear it. There are these big gaps between doing things. Like waiting for someone to get off the telephone. Or waiting for the bus. What do you do with that time?

Like washing the dishes; you can be just as functional and be in a space of melody. In fact, I think the melody can even enhance the experience of actually doing it. You can actually be more in it. For me, oftentimes, it will bring me into a place where, oh, the resentments for having to do material kinds of things might go away. It makes it more pleasant; it makes it into a sense that I am actually doing a ritual that can be a positive spiritual experience, even if it's just washing the dishes.[3]

When I'm driving through the countryside or walking in a lovely place, I find that the tones rise up out of me spontaneously. I was walking in the woods near the Northern California coast with a friend, and we decided to lie down under a huge wild bay leaf tree. We agreed to be silent, attuning to the energy of the tree. But after a few minutes, something irrepressible arose within my throat, and I just had to tone. I didn't warn him. I just let loose with this incredible full lovely tone. And then I was quiet again.

Within a few minutes, the woods that had been totally silent were filled with birdsong. Birds of all kinds flocked to the bay tree while squirrels and chipmunks ran back and forth along its branches. We were amazed that the wild creatures seemed to be attracted to the sound. It was as if they knew that we were one of them and that we, too, could sing out just for the pleasure of it.

———————

I read somewhere that birds sing in order to declare their territory—as if there were no other reason why birds sang! Having spent a great deal of time in the woods, and a lot of time observing birds, I believe that they also sing to keep in touch with each other as they travel. At sunrise and sunset, virtually every bird in the neighborhood can be observed, perching in the highest trees, simply sitting there—facing the sun—and singing. This is clearly not a time for declaring territory! It's just a time for kicking back and singing, for the pure joy of it.

We would do well to emulate the birds. One of the greatest joys that we can experience is to be among other people, ideally in nature, expressing our pleasure through sound, spontaneously blending our sounds in harmony. This can be one of the highest expressions of our spirituality.

———————

My friends and I love to tone at parties, group gatherings, meditations, and just about anywhere, anytime. When we raise our voices together, the effect is often magical and wonderful.

When my sons (who are now grown) were infants, I enjoyed spontaneously singing, humming, and droning to them as they fell asleep. But as they became older and more susceptible to peer pressure and concepts of what is "normal," they began to object to my strange sounds.

When they were teenagers, as I was learning about toning, I would often made these vibratory sounds while I was in the shower or meditating.

The boys generally learned to put up with their strange mother. They knew they could depend on me to heal their aches and pains with herbs and crystals—without getting into those weird sounds.

My older son, Kalon, went off to college, and he'd been gone for six months when I went to visit him. He was feeling overwhelmed with pressure from final exams and a traumatic relationship that had recently ended. I offered to do a *Vibrational Alignment* for him, which he accepted.

During that treatment, I toned to help him release pressure that had built up at several chakras. To my surprise—and his—he joined me. As a child, he sang off-key, and vocalizing was not something that ordinarily gave him much pleasure. With toning, however, there are no mistakes. You simply make the sounds that feel good to you. This was the first time he experienced the power of his voice, and he was amazed by how good it felt.

After that session—which did wonders to improve his energy and his attitude—he found himself toning in the shower and around his apartment. It was a terrific release of tension for him. Eventually he bought a guitar, took voice lessons, and began writing his own songs, which are a unique blend of toning and singing.

My younger son, Reuben, was still in high school and not inclined to doing anything terribly unconventional—like toning. When his older brother came home from college for Christmas vacation, I invited a small group of close friends for an after-Christmas party. Ordinarily, Reuben would go off and "do his own thing" after dinner, but on this evening I was determined to find something that would be entertaining for all of us.

I remembered a "levitation" experiment and thought it would be fun to try. Reuben allowed himself to be persuaded to join us. One of my guests— a man of 180 pounds—sat in a straight-backed chair while four people (including my two sons and myself) stood by each leg of the chair. Each person folded his or her hands together with the index fingers extended. These pairs of fingers were then inserted under the man's armpits and under his knees. Then the four of us tried to lift him—without straining in any way.

Predictably, we could barely lift the fellow. His arms went up, and his knees went up, but his bottom only raised about an inch and we promptly brought him down again.

Then each of us took our right hand and held it, palm down, over the top of his head. Then we added our left hands, in the same manner, so there were eight hands above his head. We held our hands that way for about two minutes in silence, and then we resumed our previous positions at the corners of his chair.

When we tried to lift him the second time, a remarkable thing happened. We exerted exactly the same effort, but this time we lifted my guest about two feet into the air! A gasp of surprise went round the room, including my hefty guest who was suspended mid-air, and my two sons whose fingers were under his armpits.

After we lowered him, Kalon conjectured that if we did the same gesture with our hands while toning, this might create an even more powerful effect. It sounded like fun, so the four of us once again put our hands above my guest's head and this time we toned for two minutes. I don't believe that Reuben had ever toned before. Then we tried again and, to our amazement, we lifted our hefty guest nearly up to the ceiling! The difference was astounding.

Reuben was so impressed that he insisted we try the same experiment with the hide-a-bed. He knew how heavy it was, having helped move it into the house. We were all skeptical but, being full of Christmas spirit, we agreed to try. As you can imagine, on our first effort, we could barely budge the heavy piece of furniture.

We all moved in toward the center of the hide-a-bed and put our hands above each other's in the prescribed fashion. When we assumed our positions and tried again, the hide-a-bed actually went up a couple inches.

We came together a second time, and repeated the same gesture while toning full blast for several minutes. We each returned to our corners and unbelievably, the hide-a-bed went up over a foot into the air, suspended merely by our index fingers! Every furniture mover should learn this technique!

The rest of the evening we sat around, enthusiastically toning and chanting. It was a great party.

So why does this work? Perhaps it's about joining our energies. When we all tone in harmony, this helps to bring us into alignment with each other. If we can actually transcend the force of gravity with a simple party game, just think of what we can do when we join our voices and our intentions together.

Exercise: "Levitation" with Toning

One person (let's call her Lucia) sits in a straight-backed chair. One person stands by each leg of the chair. Those standing fold their hands together with the index fingers extended (reminiscent of the second hand position in the game that goes, "This is the church, this is the steeple...").

The two people standing at Lucia's shoulders insert their joined index fingers under her armpits (from behind). The two people standing at her knees insert their joined index fingers just under her bent knees (from the outside). Then the four individuals try to lift her—without straining.

Each person takes his or her right hand and holds it, palm down, over the top of Lucia's head. No hand touches her head nor the other hands, but the four hands are layered one on top of the other above her head. Then each person adds his or her left hand, so there are eight hands above her head.

The hands are held that way for one minute in silence. Resuming the previous positions, with joined index fingers under armpits and knees, try to lift her again, without straining.

Return to the eight-handed position. Be silent for a minute. As you feel inspired, begin to tone spontaneously. Just let the sound arise from within. Make any sound that feels good to you, but listen to the sounds of the other people, and find a sound that feels harmonious with the other sounds. Allow your tones to blend and merge for as long as it feels good—approximately two or three more minutes. The toning will probably stop spontaneously when the time is right. (Note: this is most likely to be successful if two or more people are already comfortable with toning.)

Resume your previous positions, with joined index fingers under her armpits and knees. Try to lift her again, without straining in any way.

This is a marvelous exercise to do at parties or workshops.

Exercise: Improvising Gibberish

This exercise will help you to loosen up your voice, express your feelings and learn how to improvise. Ideally, it should be done with two or more people, though you can play around with gibberish on your own.

Some people find that it is remarkably difficult to do this exercise at first, because it sounds like baby talk. The trick is to get over your inhibitions and give yourself permission to be idiotic. If the person who begins is willing to be silly, this will help the others to loosen up.

The first person (let's call her Sonja) makes loud and very clearly enunciated vowel sounds with exaggerated movements of

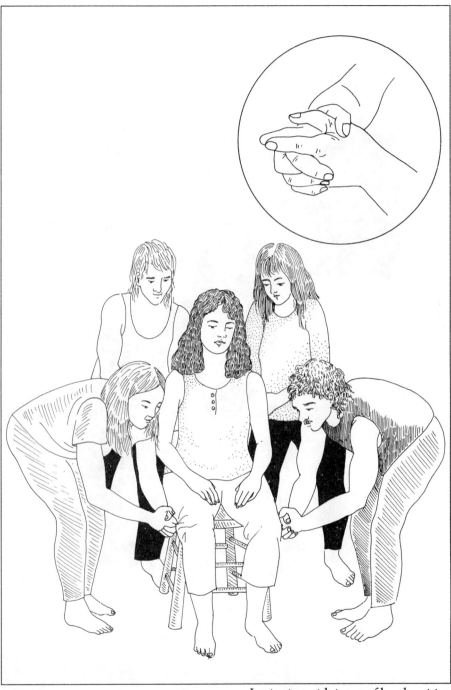

Levitation with insert of hand position

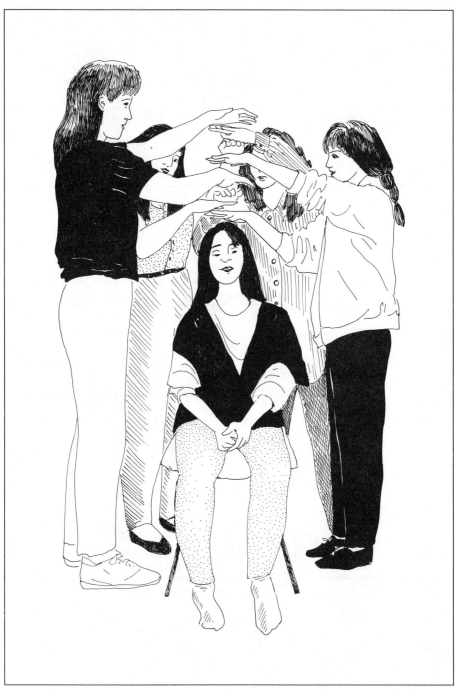

Eight-handed position for levitation

the mouth. After each vowel, the second person (let's call him Marty) imitates Sonja and makes the same exaggerated vowel sound: A, E, I, O, U (OO).

Sonja adds a consonant onto the vowels, and makes loud, exaggerated vowel-and-consonant sounds (always just one syllable at a time). Marty imitates each of Sonja's sounds: AIM, EEL, ICE, OM, OOG.

Sonja adds new consonants onto the vowels: AID, EAR, AISLE, OAK, BLUE.

Marty adds his own consonants onto the vowels: ACHE, EEP, FIRE, BLOW, BOO.

Sonja starts talking in three-syllable sets, emphasizing the first and third syllables, keeping up a constant rhythm. She pretends to be saying something in this non-sensical gibberish, which sounds like pig-Latin. She is very dramatic, emotional, and silly—as if she were really trying to express something.

For example, Sonja shakes her finger in Marty's face and says: "Pa-da-no ma-ty-ko!"

Marty responds with indignation: "Da-ma-ko. Fen-de-tu!" holding up his fist.

Now Sonja puts out her lower lip and looks offended. Her voice is suddenly very sweet. "Na-ka-na na-ka-na. Den-de-ka. Do-ne-de."

After doing this for awhile, one of the partners breaks into song and begins singing his or her dialogue like an opera. The other partner responds, and they are soon doing a dramatic duet. By this time you may want to drop the three-syllable rhythm and get into free-form. Continue in this fashion until you both feel finished.

Thanks to Chava Lasson for this exercise.

Exercise: Group Toning

Whenever a group is gathered together—for a party, meditation, workshop or just a family gathering, you have the potential to enjoy group toning. It is not necessary that people have any previous experience at toning, though it helps.

Toning is a way of adding another dimension to whatever is already happening. When I gather with my friends, we like to form a circle and tone together. Joining hands in a circle, which brings our energies together, we put our right hands with the palms down (because most of us give out more energy with our right hands) and our left hands with the palms up (because most of us are more receptive on the left side). This creates a weaving of energy within the circle in which each participant is both giving and receiving energy.

Decide what kind of toning you're going to use and instruct the group accordingly. There are three main choices. Your group may want to: (1) tone simultaneously, with everyone beginning each tone at the same time and holding it as long as possible and then waiting until everyone is ready to begin the next tone, or (2) tone simultaneously, with everyone beginning each tone at the same time and holding it only until most of the other people have stopped or (3) start whenever you feel inspired, hold the tone as long as you wish, and then start up again so the tones overlap.

The first two methods tend to create overtones which can be extremely rich and rewarding. The latter method keeps the sound going constantly without pause and this can create an intense and pleasing effect. In any case, eventually the group will find its own completion and the tones will taper off. Some groups continue for just a few minutes and others go on for ten or more minutes. One person can guide the group. This is one format that you might use.

> Inhale and bring in the highest quality of air, the prana, through your nose. Exhale through your mouth and release the tension. Do this ten times. [Pause.]

> Now go within and notice: How does your body feel? Are you fatiqued? Is your body tight anywhere? Do you feel loose and joyful? In a minute, I'm going to ask you to make some sounds to express your feelings. These might not be pleasant sounds. Just use your voice to release the tension of the day. Feel free to groan or moan or sigh. No screaming, please. Otherwise, just let go and release for a few minutes. Just begin and end at your own pace. [Pause for a few minutes to let people release. Be sure to do this yourself.]

> Let's be quiet now and breathe deeply. Inhale and bring that breath all the way down to your abdomen. Feel the abdomen expanding. Let your breath be so strong that your neighbor can hear you inhaling and exhaling. [Pause for a minute.]

> Now go inside and feel your essence. You might experience it as energy or color. Try to express your essence as sound. Don't think about it—just open up your mouth and let the sound come out, and as you do this, listen to the group sound, and see if you can bring your sound in harmony with the group sound. [Continue with this sounding for at least a few minutes until the group finds its own harmony. If the energy is good, you might want to go on for a long time.]

Exercise: Visualization with Wheel

This visualization is ideal for opening or closing a group, particularly when the spiritual energy is strong. Form a circle and hold hands, as described in "Group Toning."

Inhale and bring in the highest quality air, the prana, through your nose. Exhale through your mouth and release tension. Do this ten times. [Pause.]

Imagine that we are a wheel. The hub is at the center of our circle, and each of us is a spoke. Our joined hands create the outer rim of the wheel. Now a ray of white light is streaming onto the rim from above and it is radiating out through the spokes to each one of us. As we bring in this high, positive energy, we are charging the wheel.

Now it's getting ready to take off. Feel the wheel spinning in a counter-clockwise direction. It's rising up off the earth and spinning toward the heavens.

Let's make a tone, or a combination of tones that will power our wheel and carry it high high up into the cosmos. [Spend several minutes making tones.]

Now it's time to bring our wheel back down to earth. It's slowing down and the wheel is starting to spin in a clockwise direction. The spin is getting slower and slower as it moves toward the earth. Let's tone and bring it slowly in for a landing.

[The sounds will get deeper and the group will continue toning until it feels finished.]

We've completed a successful landing. Now we all feel re-charged and ready to enjoy the day (or the evening).

Exercise: Sensual Massage with Vocalizing

A chapter on Toning for Pure Pleasure would not be complete without sensual toning. When any kind of lovemaking is combined with sound, the pleasure can increase dramatically. Sensual massage can be a delightful part of sexual foreplay, or a sweet experience in itself.

Men often find it difficult to be receptive—to lie back and passively accept being loved, caressed, nurtured. It is even more difficult for most men to give voice to the pleasure they receive. Women, on the other hand, often purr like kittens while being massaged. Of course, there are exceptions to both these generalities. A fine way for anyone to become more adept at being receptive is to practice vocalizing during a massage.

The person giving the massage can encourage their partner to communicate when they enjoy the way they are being touched—by asking that person to make sounds. Point out that it is probably pleasureable to him (if it is a man) to make love to a woman who expresses her enjoyment through sounds. Likewise, it is a delight to the masseuse to receive positive feedback, to know without doubt that her or his loving energy is being well-received.

Tell your partner that you are going to experiment with different strokes and you want to know, through sound, which ones are pleasing. Ask your partner to notice and express the difference in sensation between these various strokes: (1) very light stroking of the hairs of the body and gentle scratching of the skin; (2) licking the skin or breathing on the skin; (3) stroking with a feather versus feathering with the fingers.

As the masseuse, you, too, can make sounds that, for you, give expression to the movements you are making. You may want to hum, to moan, to make lusty, appreciative sounds, to growl. You may serenade your partner with a song or chant. You may tone for the heart chakra or the second chakra. Ask your partner which sounds are most exciting or stimulating.

The real secret is to play and have fun.

Exercise: Toning with Tantric Lovemaking

Tantra is a form of yoga that uses a wide range of methods for channeling energy into the higher chakras. Tantric lovemaking is a form of sacred sexuality that involves channeling sexual energies through non-goal-oriented lovemaking. It may involve raising the sexual energies through the spinal column, to find release in one of the energy centers, rather than through normal orgasm and ejaculation.

The method of Tantric lovemaking which I will describe I call Tantrananda (the Joy of Tantra) and it can be used by couples or individuals. Tantrananda requires a sense of the body as an appropriate vessel for the spiritual energies, a willingness to surrender to being moved from within, and—when practiced with a partner—a deep sense of mutual trust and caring.

Non-goal-oriented lovemaking means pleasuring one's partner while temporarily avoiding genital stimulation, so that the erotic zones spread out and encompass the whole body. Thus we learn to savor the more subtle pleasures: the tender sensuality of fine touch, the warmth of skin against skin, the joy of communion with nature. This kind of sensuality leaves us feeling balanced and full, and the pleasure is deep and long-lasting and flows into our daily lives on all levels. The energy is harmonious with concentration and meditation and the required self-control is consistent with spiritual development.

This form of sacred sexuality has been practiced for centuries in India, Tibet and China. It makes use of the Kundalini—the powerful dragon-like energy that resides at the base of the spine. When Kundalini is aroused, she becomes forceful and rises up through the spine, pushing her way through each of the chakras. If the adept is highly evolved and the chakras can open to let her pass, she will eventually reach the third eye and the crown chakra where she will ignite the union of pituitary and pineal secretions, leading to an experience of bright white light. This is the state of transcendence, the sense of divine peace and oneness with the universe that is called Enlightenment or Nirvana.

There are many ways of arousing the Kundalini. One of the quickest is through the sexual embrace. Though devotees of Tantra rarely experience Enlightenment, many do taste of deep bliss when they learn to raise their sexual energy instead of spending it through ejaculation and genital orgasm.

Instead, the energy can be raised to a specific chakra and then both people can simultaneously release their energy through that chakra. This can lead, for example, to a mutual orgasm of the heart. When the heart is aroused in this way, both people may experience an incredible sense of unconditional love toward each other as well as their children, animals, friends, and anyone who crosses their path.

The energy of Kundalini cannot move through a chakra that is closed, though it may attempt to burn or force itself through, causing considerable discomfort to the person. For this reason, tantric lovemaking should be preceded by at least one year of physical and spiritual disciplines such as the practice of yoga, Tai Chi, meditation and other arts of opening the chakras.

When you feel ready to experience Tantrananda, begin by setting aside about two hours of totally uninterrupted time with your partner. Disconnect the phone and hang a "Don't Disturb" sign on your door. Better yet, find a cabin in the woods. Put on some music you both find relaxing. Remove your clothes and bring along some pleasantly scented, edible massage oil.

Take turns slowly and lovingly carressing, stroking and massaging every part of one another's bodies while avoiding the genitals and nipples. Give yourselves plenty of time. Let the person being touched express her or his pleasure by appreciative sounds or movements of the body. (See the exercise on *Toning with Sensual Massage* in this chapter.)

When you both feel fully relaxed, begin to mutually pleasure one another, still avoiding the erogenous zones. Let go of any goals. Come together and fall apart. This is a game of love in which the only rule is to do nothing until you feel moved from within. Lie separately for awhile. Concentrate on breathing at the same pace.

Perhaps your toes might touch. A timeless moment may pass and then you may find yourselves lunging for one another—devouring each other. Then you might laugh and fall away.

Breathing together and resting together, the passion builds ever so slowly. There is a sense of complete trust—in each other, and in the Spirit that moves you both. There are no manipulations, just a deep caring. And from this caring there is a flowing like water, like rivers, like endless time.

Let your mind be empty. Think of nothing—or only of your lover. Don't worry, you can do no wrong. Nothing is expected of you. You could go and get a peach and share it with your lover; everything is infused with sensuality.

You reach a point where you definitely want to touch each other intimately. If you like, the nipples and genitals may be gently caressed. But when your arousal builds to a high pitch, where ordinarily you would crave penetration and orgasm, then it's time to rechannel your energies.

This transition is a personal thing, and you'll want to find a way that feels appropriate to both of you. Perhaps one of you will gently stop and hold the other at arm's length. You may look deeply into one another's eyes.

Turn off the background music and position yourselves (lying or sitting) so that your chakras are more or less aligned, with your abdomen, chest and forehead nearly touching your partner's. Ideally your spine should be more-or-less straight. Try sitting in the yab-yum position, in which the man (if there is a man and woman) is on the bottom, with his legs in a crosslegged position (see illus. pg. 150). If necessary, his back can be supported with pillows against a wall or headboard. The woman sits on his lap, facing him, with her legs wrapped around his waist.

Look into your partner's eyes and attune to each other's breathing until you are inhaling and exhaling in unison. Tantrananda
makes use of *Color Breathing* combined with *Toning for the Chakras*,
as described in Chapter Ten. To prepare for this exercise, read the
following visualization into a tape recorder. When the time is right,
turn on the tape. Feel free to stop the exercise at any point in order
to move into elaborations of your own design.

You may find that the energy will burst forth from one of the
chakras spontaneously, and you may feel an orgasmic release through
that chakra. After experiencing orgasmic release through one chakra,
you can recharge the energy and experience release through another chakra.

When you feel ready to come back to earth, you can complete
the exercise. (Note: Tantrananda can be practiced by one person
alone by arousing, raising and releasing her or his own sexual
energy. It can also be used by same-sex partners.)

Concentrate your attention at the first chakra at the base of
your spine. Inhale and breathe the color red into your first chakra.
As you exhale, tone E as in "red," three times, with your partner. As
you tone, feel the warmth and energy in your genitals. Imagine
yourself as a great oak tree with roots extending from your tailbone,
going deep down into the earth. Feel the sap rising through your
roots and up your trunk, into your spine.

Bring the energy into your second chakra, below your navel.
Think of an orange or apricot and inhale this color into your pelvic
area, below the navel. Tone O as in "home," three times, with your
partner. Allow the orange to spread all through your lower abdominal area. Feel it expanding your colon, letting all things flow freely.
Let go and breathe. Orange is the color of friendliness. Feel this
energy emanating from you toward others.

Inhale and bring the energy up your spine to your third chakra.
Bring the bright yellow of the sun into your solar plexus. Exhale and
tone AOM with your partner, three times, while you emanate your
own light in all directions. This is your personal power shining out
into the world. Yellow will help you to relax into love and fine
touch, without having to perform.

Inhale and bring the energy up your spine to your fourth
chakra. Visualize a green meadow and breathe that color deep into
your heart as you tone AH as in "hah," with your partner, four
times. Green is nature's way of loving you. Open your heart and let
her in. Feel your heart expanding—expanding—and relaxing. This
is the center of Universal Love and forgiveness. If you harbor

Yab-yum position

resentment toward anyone, when you exhale, release that energy. Continue doing this until your heart is free of resentment.

Inhale the green light again, and when you exhale, imagine pink light flowing from your heart and radiating out to your lover. Feel it easing away all your lover's worries and self-doubts. Hold this special being in the pink light and feel him or her opening to your love energy. Inhale green and exhale pink as you tone AH with your partner, four times.

Then let your partner be silent and receive your love and pink light on the inhale as you exhale and tone AH two times. Then you can be silent and receive your partner's love and pink light on the inhale as your partner exhales and tones AH two times.

Looking deeply into each other's eyes, continue toning AH, alternating the tone from one person to the other. You will tone AH as your partner inhales, and then your partner will tone AH as you inhale. Each of you will tone four times.

Inhale and bring the energy up your spine to the fifth chakra at the base of your neck. Visualize a beautiful blue light glowing at your neck, radiating upward and filling your whole head. Tone UU as in "blue" four times, with your partner, and feel a calm sense of peace come over you. Imagine blue light cascading like water over the top of your head, eyebrows, eyes, temples, washing away all the tension.

Inhale and bring the energy up your spine to the sixth chakra at your third eye. Feel the indigo light flooding into your inner eye as you tone MM as in "mom," four times, with your partner. Touch your third eye very gently to your partner's as you tone together. This is the center of telepathy and higher intuition. Feel yourself opening your inner eye to the God or Goddess who resides in this man or woman.

Inhale and bring the energy up to your seventh chakra. Imagine a violet flame at the crown of your head. Tone EE as in "glee" four times, with your partner. Release whatever negativity, fear, envy, jealousy, paranoia, pride, hatred or anger you may be carrying. Visualize these feelings as colors and see them going into the violet light and being transmuted into free energy. A great burden is being lifted from your body.

You can move into a state of meditation now for as long as you like. When you feel ready to come back to earth, you and your partner will tone just once, at the same time, for each chakra. Tone MM as in "mom" for the third eye while visualizing indigo. Tone

UU as in "blue" while visualizing blue. Tone AH as in "hah" while visualizing green. Tone AH again while visualizing pink. Tone AOM while visualizing yellow. Tone O as in "home" while visualizing orange. Tone E as in "red" while visualizing red.

Tantric lovemaking is a way of learning to relax and to concentrate on increasing intimacy, trust and Universal Love. It releases energies in a way that can enhance all of your relationships. It may hold the key to aging gracefully, helping us to accept each other as we are, enjoying the more subtle expressions of our tenderness. Ultimately, it becomes a tool for dying gracefully, teaching us to let go of ego gratification and to become more aware of the cosmic bliss that lies beyond.

12

TONING FOR BIRTH AND DEATH

We enter this world from the realm of the Dreamtime, and we re-enter the Dreamtime as we leave this world. The guide who sits by us as we go between worlds is a precious being, a midwife of birth at one end of the spectrum, and a midwife of death at the other. If we are fortunate, we will be guided through these transitions by a humble person who can step back and allow the process to evolve in its own time, at its own rhythm.

Toning for Pregnancy and Childbirth

The good vibrations of your songs and tones will be felt by your little one from the beginning. After the fifth month *in utero*, this precious being will be able to hear you.[1] Talk, sing and tone to your baby throughout your pregnancy, and encourage the baby's father to talk and sing also. This excerpt was taken from my book, *Healing Yourself During Pregnancy*.

We tend to think that a baby in utero is entirely cut off from the world that lies just beyond a thin layer of skin. We seldom consider the child within as a conscious being, capable of responding to sounds, emotions, and the inner environment that its mother creates through her sense of well-being, or lack of it.

In his excellent book, *The Secret Life of the Unborn Child*, Dr. Thomas Verny tells...a remarkable story about a cello player who found that he knew certain pieces even before he had read the music. When he described this to his mother (also a cello player), she remarked that those were the pieces she had played most frequently while she was pregnant with him.

One of my clients told me that there were certain passages from the Bible that he dearly loved and easily learned by heart. Later his mother told him that those were the passages that she had read aloud, over and over, during her pregnancy with him.

Verny tells about a woman who found her two-year-old daughter sitting on the living room floor chanting to herself, "Breathe in, breathe out, breathe in, breathe out" in exactly the same pattern that her mother had used for her Lamaze exercises all through her pregnancy and delivery—and not at all since.

With my first child, I was in labor for thirty-six hours. The last several hours were filled with painful contractions. I had been trained in the Lamaze method, and I made good use of the pant-and-blow technique which consists of three short pants followed by a long blow. For several days after my son was born, he had a peculiar habit of taking three short pants followed by a long blow!....

Modern research with plants shows that they like to be spoken to, and they respond well to certain music, and grow more profusely when they're loved and well cared for. If this is true for a plant, it must be doubly true for the growing human baby.

Here's a special note for fathers:

When your partner becomes pregnant, be sure to stroke her belly and speak to your baby. Studies have shown that the unborn child actually hears its father's voice in utero, and when a father has spoken soothingly to his baby before birth, the newborn is able to pick out his father's voice in a room. And if the baby is crying, the father's soothing voice can comfort the baby and help it to stop crying. [2]

While her close friend, Charlotte, was pregnant, Ilianna Culvert-Dufford, a toning practitioner from San Jose, California, often came and toned through her cupped hands into her friend's belly. She was present at Willow's birth and had the opportunity to hold the infant after Willow nursed for the first time. Rocking the baby gently in her arms, Ilianna toned to welcome her into the world. Hearing the familiar tone, baby Willow's eyes opened wide with a look of blissful recognition.

Before Willow could speak, she and Ilianna would communicate through toning, Willow playing a game with sounds and cooing in harmony with "Auntie Illie." When she was two, she and her mother were at a gathering at Ilianna's home. The adults got together in the living room to tone, and Willow ran to Ilianna's side, cuddled up close and wouldn't be coaxed away. She wanted to tone with the woman who was the first to bring her the gift of song.

Toning can be used even before conception, when there is difficulty conceiving or holding a pregnancy. I was doing a *Vibrational Alignment* for Betty, a close friend who has had several miscarriages during the first month or two of pregnancy, and she wanted desperately to have a child. I felt that her second chakra energy was very weak (see Chapter Ten). After doing some counseling related to the underlying cause of this weakness—which involved her mother's inability to accept Betty as a sexual being—I felt a lot of anger coming from her, and I suggested that we do some screaming. She was glad to do that, and grateful to have me join her. We both screamed for several minutes, and she felt a tremendous release.

I felt the impulse to lie next to her, belly to belly, second chakra to second chakra, and to tone for her. (An alternate method would have been to cup my hands over her belly and tone into my cupped hands.) Betty was comfortable with my suggestion, so we lay together, belly to belly, while I toned deep tones and she joined me. At some point, the tones merged and it felt like being inside a cave with echoing overtones reverberating against the walls.

After several minutes, I got up and felt the energy at her second chakra; it had become strong and full. At the end of the *Vibrational Alignment,* I felt a wild impulse to break out singing,

> Someone's in the kitchen with Dinah,
> Someone's in the kitchen I know-o-o-o.
> Someone's in the kitchen with Dinah,
> Strummin' on the old banjo.

It turned out her mother's name was Dinah (I hadn't known that), and this was a song that she and her Mother loved to sing. So we had a good laugh, and it was a rollicking way to end our session. Shortly after this treatment, Betty became pregnant again. She called me last week, delighted, and said she was at the end of her first trimester. "We just got back from the doctor and we heard the baby's heartbeat. This one's a keeper!"

Diane came to my Toning Workshop while she was pregnant, and when she learned the sounds that correspond to the vagina (first chakra) and uterus (second chakra), she found it felt very pleasant to make these low, deep, resonant sounds. She practiced them regularly throughout the day and discovered that if she made these deep sounds while moving her bowels, it helped her anus to relax, so the movement was easier.

Diane had her first baby by cesarean. She tried to have her second baby vaginally, but her cervix would not dilate sufficiently, so she was forced to have her second by cesarean. When she became pregnant with her third child, she was determined to have this baby vaginally. She heard that midwives encourage women to keep their mouths open during the last stage of labor, since this helps to open up the vagina. She reasoned that the best way to keep her mouth open would be by toning. Her labor coach was supportive of this plan.

Contrary to the doctor's advice, she waited until she went into labor, and then she went to the hospital where her midwife joined her. When she was examined, she was 4 cm. dilated. Diane started making low, deep vibratory tones, and within *one hour* she was 10 cm. dilated, and gave birth vaginally and effortlessly.

Labor is an activity that mother and baby do simultaneously, and it can proceed far more smoothly if mother and unborn child are consciously aware of each other and working together. I encourage mothers to tune in on their babies; to talk and sing to them while they are in labor, so that their babies will feel reassured, and there will be a sense of teamwork between mother and child.

Linda's birth was my first opportunity to experience this first-hand. Linda was understandably anxious and worried when I arrived to give her support; her labor was going slowly. While we waited for the midwife, I encouraged her to focus on her baby. I told her about three-year-old Jason, who became indignant when he heard his mother talk about "her" labor. "Mom!" he said forcefully, "It was *our* labor! I did just as much work as you did!" I felt certain that he was right. Through a *rebirthing* process, I had re-experienced my own birth, and I re-lived being stuck inside my mother's birth canal. My mother told me she had been "knocked out" toward the end of her labor, but she never knew why. I had a first-hand re-memory of feeling as if I were going to die, feeling totally abandoned by my mother, and then being delivered by forceps. That *rebirthing* experience, combined with Jason's comment to his mother, made me wonder if I felt abandoned because I lost the psychic connection with my mother when she was under anaesthesia.

I encouraged Linda to turn her attention toward her belly, stroking it lovingly, and speaking with encouragement to her baby. The results were even more spectacular than I had hoped for.

Linda started chanting to her baby, "Come on, Baby! Come on, Baby! You can do it!" She was stroking her belly, working *with* her baby, so they were laboring *together* to produce this birth. Within minutes, Linda calmed down. As she reassured her baby, her own anxiety passed. Her words became a mantra: "Come on, Baby. You can do it. Come on, Baby. You can do it." The more she said it, the more she believed it.

Soon she was totally absorbed in nurturing and stroking her baby/belly, and by the time the midwife arrived, the contractions had picked up and the midwife reported that she was dilating nicely. Within another hour, her baby girl was born easily and happily.

In France, childbirth educator Frederick Leboyer is now encouraging women to sing while in labor.[3] Breath and sound can be used in other ways to assist childbirth. The following passage is taken from my book, *Healing Yourself During Pregnancy*. This section was written in collaboration with Cathrin Prince Leslie, midwife.

As her labor progresses, a woman who is encouraged to express herself freely may make sounds similar to having a prolonged orgasm. During delivery she may scream in pain or in rapture. These sounds help to open and relax her pelvis and her cervix. Yet there are few places where such "uncivilized" noises are encouraged. A supportive attendant can encourage such behavior. The mother can discuss her fears openly. She can cry or scream or do whatever she needs to do without fear of being judged.

Many people are shy about using their voices forcefully, so practice using your voice whenever you get a chance. Sing along with the songs on the stereo. When you're in the shower, sing out at the top of your lungs. You'll find it feels good, and you may even get a few laughs!

Exercise: Vibrating Your Womb

This exercise is taken from my book, *Healing Yourself During Pregnancy*, from the chapter on Labor and Birth, written in collaboration with Cathrin Prince Leslie.

When you get into a situation of anxiety that causes you to tighten up, your breathing usually changes....

When you find yourself feeling tense, observe your breath. You'll probably find that you're holding your breath or breathing in a very shallow way. Of course, holding your breath deprives you of oxygen, and just increases your tension. Try taking a deep breath, and as you exhale, make a sound like "heh" or "hoh" from deep in your chest, and hold it for the length of the exhalation.

Now inhale and exhale again, making the sound, and think of the vibrations of that sound moving to any part of your body where you are holding tesnion. Inhale and exhale again, making the deep sound, and feel your breath and the sound carrying away any possible tension, anger, or tightness.

Now inhale and feel how good it is to take in a fresh breath of air. Then exhale, and make a deep sound and think of the vibration of that sound moving through your womb, through your cervix, and out your vagina, opening and releasing and making way for your baby.

During labor, remember that instead of holding your breath and trying to block out the pain, tune into the pain, inhale deeply, and as you exhale, make a sound that expresses what you are feeling: moan, groan, sigh, wail, or scream. Allow yourself to become primitive and animalistic.[4]

The Midwifery of Death

The passage into life and the passage out of life are remarkably similar, and require similar reassurances. The role of assistant at either end of the spectrum is a great honor to perform, and certainly one of the highest spiritual experiences, if we can but take the time to participate fully.

Unfortunately, the fear of death frequently colors both experiences, so that we are cut off from being truly present by the intervention of tubes and machinery. Vocal sound is one way that we can reclaim the experience of the sacred passage.

I have often had the opportunity to use sound as a part of the rituals surrounding the end of life's journey. I first grew aware of the importance of this form of nonverbal communication when I attended Elisabeth Kubler-Ross's five-day "Life, Death and Transition Workshop." One of many ways that she taught us the importance of nonverbal communication was to have us sing together at the beginning and end of each day. We sang all kinds of songs: silly songs, mushy songs, old, sentimental songs. We sang songs that aroused laughter and songs that brought tears. Some of our songs were personal and full of memories. I sang "Good Night, Irene," because it reminded me of being a little girl when my father was driving cross-country late at night in the old Cadillac, singing "Good Night, Irene," to keep himself awake at the wheel.

I enjoyed these group sings, and I was disappointed when the second workshop that I attended turned out to be remarkably unmusical. Despite our efforts, we couldn't seem to get a coherant group sound. During that second workshop, I became friendly with Jason (not his real name), a thirty-five-year-old musician who was in the last stages of melanoma, a cancer that spreads throughout the body. On the first day of the workshop he could barely sit up, but he spoke briefly about his illness and about his anger and pain at being unable to communicate with his father. On the second day, he was only with us for an hour before he was taken to a private room to rest. After lunch, the attendant told us that Lawrence was dying.

Elisabeth suggested that we could go as a group (there were seventy-five of us) to stand outside his room and sing. The thought of bringing this painfully unmusical group to sing at the doorway of our dying friend didn't seem too appealing to me, and yet not a single person held back. We moved as a unit, motivated by the feeling that "Ah! Here is something that we can *do* to possibly help this young man!" Within minutes, our group of seventy-five people had settled into the narrow hallway outside Lawrence's room, and we began to sing.

This group that had been so dissonant just hours before was suddenly singing in nearly perfect harmony. We sounded good! It brought tears to my eyes! It was a joy to sing for our friend.

We sang song after song, filling the building with vibrant sound. Then Elisabeth's assistant came out of Jason's room and signaled us to stop. He spoke to us in a quiet voice. "Jason's heart rate got stronger after your first song, and shortly after that he sat up. He's feeling stronger, and he's decided to visit his father. We've arranged for him to leave on the next plane."

While I was living in British Columbia, I studied Gestalt and Reiki with Bethal Phaigh, a wonderful woman in her seventies who had been a friend and student of Fritz Perls (the father of Gestalt Therapy). Her life work was the integration of Gestalt with the teachings of the Hawaiian Kahunas. I loved this woman and it was painful to see her dying of breast and bone cancer. Yet I knew that she was at peace with dying, and it was her time to go.

During the last months, those of us who studied with Bethel were honored to help her through her transition. She had truly been a mother to so many of us who felt misunderstood by our own parents. She had given us the unconditional love that we so desperately needed from an older person. And we were the loving children to this precious woman—whose own children had been unable to understand the unconventional lifestyle that she had chosen in her later years.

During her last week of life, she was in a lot of pain, and she no longer wanted to speak, which often happens in the last days. So her care-givers turned to songs. Bethel always encouraged her students to sing at workshops, so they sang the songs they had learned from her. Their favorite was the one that always brought tears at the end of the workshops. It is sung to the tune of "Rose, Rose, Rose," and you fill in the name of the person you are singing to.

> Dear Bethal, Dear Bethal,
> Let me tell you how I feel:
> You have given me such pleasure,
> I love you so!

There is a time when words cannot express the depth of our love. Then a familiar song can speak to the heart in a way that is incredibly comforting.

I remembered this several years later when I found out that my Dad had Alzheimer's Disease. When I went to visit him, I took the tape recorder. His memory was fading fast, but I encouraged him to sing the songs he could remember.

Five years later, when he could barely walk or talk and sometimes didn't even recognize me, I brought that tape to the convalescent home. He was sitting in his wheelchair when I arrived, hardly able to keep from nodding out. His eyes were glazed, and he didn't notice when I walked in and turned off the television. The woman who took care of him said he was now completely unable to communicate. She shook her head sadly. I set up the tape recorder and turned it on. "Who is that?" The words came out of his mouth with perfect clarity. I told him it was himself, and he shook his head in disbelief. But he perked up and became more energetic and he pursed his lips to kiss me—which was a sure sign that he recognized me.

I put my arm around him and encouraged him to stand up. When I used to visit him, I would get him to lean his weight on me and we would go for short walks together. We hadn't been able to do that for the last few visits, but now he was taking short little steps with me again. So I took my Dad for his last walk down the driveway of the convalescent home. While we walked together, I sang "Good Night, Irene," and every time I came to the chorus, my Dad hummed along with me.

———————

Therese Shroeder-Sheker, chairman of the music department at Regis College in Denver, practices what she calls "musical sacramental midwifery." She has created a degree program in music thanatology (thanatology means knowledge of death), in which she teaches students to use voice, harps and bells to comfort the terminally ill.

Shroeder-Sheker was interviewed by Kurt Rosenberg in *Common Boundary* Magazine. She explained that in medieval times, French monks used such music to "unbind" pain for monks who were dying. Her own mission began when she was working as a nurse's aide in a geriatric home. Acting intuitively, out of a deep desire to comfort a man who was dying from advanced emphysema—a disease that makes the exhalation of breath exceedingly difficult—she climbed into bed behind him and aligning her chest with his, she rocked him in her arms while she sang Gregorian chants and hymns.

"Everything changed," she recalls. "He had been so frightened that he was thrashing around, and his arms and legs were flailing.

The minute the rocking and singing began, he stopped flailing; it was like he drifed into sleep. He breathed the longest sigh I ever heard and he died in my arms .... that night .... I knew I wanted to be there for everybody who dies. I thought it was incredibly vulgar that someone should die with the television on. I knew no one should die alone."

Now this angel of mercy sings and plays her harp for people who are terminally ill.

"Almost everyone who is conscious will turn to me and mumble, 'You don't know how much this helps me.' Many times people have turned to me and said, 'This is the first time I've been without pain in three months.' "[5]

Talia Rose uses sound healing, sometimes accompanied by a harp, to help people make transitions, including the transition out of the physical body and into the spiritual body. She told me a story about when she was working with her friend, Steven, a musician who had AIDS.

I worked with him for over a year and saw him regularly, toning for him. Then I didn't see him for a number of months. I knew that he was preparing to leave his body, and I had a resistance to seeing him, because it was so difficult to say goodbye.

One day I suddenly got this inner message, really strong, and it said, "Go see Steven immediately. You must go see him." The date was February 13, 1989.

I called up and talked to his caretaker and he said, "Yes, you must come right now."

So I went over to his house and I walked in and he was lying in bed, looking really emaciated, and his caretaker said, "He's been in transition for over a month. We know that he wants to leave, but he hasn't quite been able to let go."

I went up to him and sat down on his bed. He opened his eyes and looked at me and said, "Good, I'm glad you're here. Put your hand on my heart and sing." That's what I did. I put my hand on his heart and I sang, and he was lying there and receiving and after a few minutes he said, "Thank you. That's enough."

I got up to leave and he said, "By the way, it's really something out there—it's like Star Trek."

I walked out the door and went home, and the next day, very

early in the morning, I got a call from his caretaker—it was February 14th, Valentine's Day. "I just wanted to tell you that Steven passed away, very peacefully, at dawn."[6]

Toning to Soothe

The last days and nights before a person leaves his or her body can be very difficult for the family, and for those who are assisting. The family doesn't want to leave the bedside for a minute, knowing that their loved one may depart at any time. Yet fatique sets in and it is best if family members can get some sleep. A hospice worker or friend who is close to the family can be indispensable at such times.

Whether you are a member of the family, or assisting, you are likely to find yourself wondering how to comfort a person who is drifting in and out of a dream-like state, who has been mostly non-verbal, and who may be heavily drugged for pain. I have found that sitting by the bedside of dying persons and holding their hands while aligning my breathing with theirs can be very comforting to them. Their breaths are often very labored and difficult to imitate, but once I am inside of their rhythm, this seems to comfort them. Perhaps it makes them feel that they are not alone.

Then I will begin breathing in blue light and sending it to the patient while toning UU as in "blue" (see Chapter Ten). This ethereal sound tends to be soothing to people who are hovering in this in-between place.

As a hospice worker, I sat by an elderly woman's deathbed, and whenever she became restless, I would hold her hand or put my hand on her forehead, which helped a little. Then I would tone UU very softly (it couldn't be heard outside the room), and she would settle down at once. But once, when her medication began to wear off, she opened her eyes and looked at me as if to say, "What is that weird noise you're making?"

I realized that her conscious mind could not accept the sound, even though her body (and presumably, her subconscious mind) had responded favorably to the sound. So I reserved the sound for when she was dozing.

A person doesn't need to be dying to benefit from the soothing effects of this exercise. Try it for anyone who is feeling agitated—as long as they are open-minded. Keep toning until they feel calm. You can use a blue light in a room where someone is agitated or dying—particularly at night, or when they're restless.

If you practice on your friends, you'll feel less shy about trying it if and when you find yourself in the presence of someone who is dying, or in an emergency. It was the best thing I could offer, and truly helpful, when I found myself at the scene of an automobile accident on a back country road, waiting an hour for the paramedics to arrive while trying to comfort a woman who had her leg pinned inside the car.

> Each time you inhale, imagine blue light coming down from the heavens. Absorb it into your own body through your neck chakra. When you exhale, fix it there, until you feel full of blue light. Then you're ready to inhale the blue and when you exhale, imagine sending it out through your third eye, bathing that person in blue. See it sweeping over him or her like ocean waves. Each time you exhale, make the sound UU as in "blue" as you send out the blue light. In your mind's eye, wrap this person in a light blue blanket of light.

Times of War and Peace

Traditionalists of the Wind River Shoshone, the Coast Salish Indians, and the Huichol Indians of Mexico, believe that the chokecherries and salmon will not come back in abundance and the sun won't rise unless they chant their prayers and perform their rituals. Westerners tend to look upon these people as being superstitious, cut off from reality.[7,8,9]

Yet when the last Traditionalist Shoshone, the last Traditionalist Coast Salish Indian and the last Traditionalist Huichol Indian—not to mention the Hopi, the Australian Aborigines and others—are wiped off the face of the earth, along with the last great trees and the last oil reserves ... will it surprise us if the chokecherries do not bloom, if the salmon do not return, and if major catastrophes occur that could lead to the sun not rising or (as the Hopi predict) the moon turning the color of blood?

All the original cultures have prophecies about a time when disasters will occur on this planet. It is a universal Judgment Day. The Hopi Religious and Spiritual Leaders have stated that the day we entered the War in Iran was the beginning of the prophecied Purification Time.[10]

For most North Americans, the song and the dance are gone from their lives, and the energy is dead. Life is all about money: dead paper scalped off of proud, tall trees, and precious metals gutted out of pure sacred places.

Living on this planet today, we are at a painful and thrilling turning point, in which we can either move toward a caring, soulful way of life, discovering our own inner personal and communal songs, crying out for Guidance and Miracles, or we can turn our hearts and souls toward death, oblivion and numbness forever.

These are the only choices. That is the beauty of these hard times, and I expect that even harder times are coming. If you are soul-dead, you will probably not survive. No amount of money will help you when things get really tough. So it's a good idea for us to tune up our miracle tools now, because we're probably going to need them.

Some of the prophecies tell us that after the Judgment Day, the people who survive will have one language and one religion and will live in peace and harmony with one another. Toning is a universal language that can be understood by all people. It is a good beginning.

If we can enter into and influence the web of electromagnetic energies that is called the Dreamtime, then we may become intelligent and active participants in this Cosmic Drama. Then we may be able to work the miracles that have been the domain of the initiates in the past. We can begin by sending out our Prayers for World Peace.

Exercise: Prayers for World Peace

Form a group of people, and begin by agreeing on a prayer or affirmation and a visualization, which could include a color and tone (see *Color Breathing* in Chapter Ten). It is not necessary to use crystals as part of this meditation, but if you have them, do not underestimate their power to amplify your thoughts and your tones and to help create the kind of reality that you are projecting.

Place a projector crystal where it can be seen by the group. This is a single-terminated crystal that stands up by itself, without support. The projector gathers and holds energy and then directs that energy into the noosphere (the atmosphere of ideas that surrounds the planet). During the meditation, each person holds their individual crystal pointing toward the projector crystal, charging it with their thoughts and energies.

Sit in a circle and follow the instructions in Chapter Eleven under *Group Toning*. Tone OM as a group, with each person finding the pitch that feels best to them. If there is plenty of time, let go of hands and do *Toning for the Chakras* as described in Chapter Ten, until you reach the the crown chakra. Sit in silence for at least five minutes and begin your visualizations.

If you're praying for peace in a particular part of the world, visualize a map of that area and send the green light of love along with the sound AH for the heart chakra, and then send the calming blue light along with the tone U.

Visualize those who are in power. Tone AH for the heart chakra and send them the pink light of love which melts away aggression.

For those who are suffering from death and loss, who are in crisis, or who are dying of starvation, flood their hearts with pink and green light and send the tone AH. Send blue and tone U to calm them and ease their pain.

This may be a good time to use the Seed Sounds described in Chapter Six. As you experiment with these sounds, you may learn how to use them as the Aborigines do, to increase and decrease energies before they manifest.

Follow your heart and continue your meditation in whatever way feels appropriate. Before you close, encourage everyone to speak from his or her heart and express appreciation out loud. When we remember to give thanks, we attract miracles.

If you used *Toning for the Chakras*, in the beginning, come back down through the chakras now, with one tone for each chakra. You can end with *The Expanded A-O-M*, as described in Chapter Ten. When your meditation is complete, join hands and let everyone hold their clasped hands up in the air and shake their hands all together and cry out, "BE HAPPY!" It is an excellent way to end a meeting—or a book.

SONGS AND CHANTS

Here is a collection of some of my favorite chants and songs. These are an assorted collection of Sufi Chants, American Indian Chants, Shaker Rounds, Tibetan Chants, Hindu Chants and Negro Spirituals and Christian Hymns.

Opening Up
I am opening up in sweet surrender
to the luminous love light of the One.

I am opening up in sweet surrender
to the luminous love light of the One.

I am opening, I am opening.
I am opening, I am opening.

The Earth Is Our Mother
The earth is our mother
we must take care of her.
The earth is our mother
we must take care of her.
Heh yun-ga hoh yun-ga heh yung-yung
Heh yun-ga hoh yun-ga heh yung-yung

'Tis sacred ground we walk upon
with every step we take.
'Tis sacred ground we walk upon
with every step we take.
Heh yun-ga hoh yun-ga heh yung-yung
heh yun-ga hoh yun-ga heh yung-yung

Listen, Listen, Listen
Listen, listen, listen
to my heart's song.
Listen, listen, listen
to my heart's song.
I will never forget thee
I will never forsake thee
I will never forget thee
I will never forsake thee.

Wearing My Long Tail Feathers
Wearing my long tail feathers as I fly
Wearing my long tail feathers as I fly
I circle around
I circle around
The boundaries of the earth.

Around the universe.

It's in Every One of Us
It's in every one of us
to be wise.
Find your heart,
open up both your eyes.
We can all know everything
without ever knowing why.
It's in every one of us
you and I.

It's in every one of us
to be free.
Find your heart,
open your eyes and see.
We can all have everything
without ever knowing how.
It's in every one of us,
here and now.

Where We Walk Is Holy
Where we (walk) is holy,
holy is the ground.
Mountain, forest, river,
listen to the sound.

Big wheel turning
all around me.
Ya-yay ya-yay ya-yay ya-yay
Ya-yay ya-yay ya-yay ya-yay
Ya-yay ya-yay ya-yay ya-yay
Ya-yay ya-yay ya-yay ya-yay
(Repeat substituting dance, sing, pray, etc. for "walk.")

I Am a Circle
I am a circle, I am healing you.
You are a circle. You are healing me.
Unite us, be as one.
Unite us, be as one.

The River
The river, she is flowing
flowing and growing —
the river, she is flowing
down to the sea.

Mother, carry me
your child I will always be.
Mother, carry me
down to the sea.

The Peace of the River
I take delight in
the peace of the river
that flows so gently
to the strength of the sea.

I take delight in
the love that keeps flowing
just like the river
between you and me.

Fly Like an Eagle
Fly like an eagle,
flying so high.
Circling the universe
on wings of pure light.

Oh, wichi-tai-o
wichi-tai-o.
Oh, wichi-tai-o
wichi-tai-o.

May we all fly like eagles.

Tibetan Prayer
Om Ah Hum Vajra Guru Padma Siddhi Hum

Mantra for Tara
Om ta-ri tu ta-ri tu-re so-ha.

Jai Ram
Sri Ram Jai Ram Jai Jai Ram
Sri Ram Jai Ram Jai Jai Ram
Sri Ram Jai Ram Jai Jai Ram
Sri Ram Jai Ram Jai Jai Ram

Hari Krishna
Hari Krishna, Hari Krishna
Krishna, Krishna, Hari, Hari
Hari Rama, Hari Rama
Rama, Rama, Hari, Hari

Chant to the Heart of Krishna
Gopala, Gopala Devakinanda Gopala
Gopala Krishna, Gopala Jai Jai
Radhar manahari, Govinda Jai Jai

Plains Wolf Dance
Hey-hey hey-hey-hey min-ga-la!
Hey-hey hey-hey-hey min-ga-la!
Hey-hey hey-hey-hey min-ga-la!
Hey-hey hey-hey-hey min-ga-la!
(Chant two times low, once high, once lower.
    Mingala is the wolf.)

I Come to the Garden
I come to the garden alone
while the dew is still on the roses
and the voice I hear, falling on my ear,
the Son of God discloses.

He walks with me,
and he talks with me,
and he tells me I am his own.
And the joy we share as we tarry there,
none other has ever known.

Amazing Grace

Amazing Grace, how sweet the sound
that saved a wretch like me.
I once was lost, but now I'm found,
was blind, but now I see.

'Twas Grace that taught my heart to fear
and Grace that fear relieved.
How precious did that Grace appear,
the hour I first believed.

Through many dangers, toils and cares
I have already come.
'Twas Grace that brought me safe this far.
'Tis Grace will lead me home.

Kum-Ba-Yah

Kum-ba-ya, my Lord, kum-ba-ya!
Kum-ba-ya, my Lord, kum-ba-ya!
Kum-ba-ya, my Lord, kum-ba-ya!
O Lord, kum-ba-ya!

Some one's singin', Lord, kum-ba-ya!
Some one's singin', Lord, kum-ba-ya!
Some one's singin', Lord, kum-ba-ya!
O Lord, kum-ba-ya!

Some one's prayin', Lord, kum-ba-ya!
Some one's prayin', Lord, kum-ba-ya!
Some one's prayin', Lord, kum-ba-ya!
O Lord, kum-ba-ya!

May the Blessings

May the blessings of the Goddess rest upon you.
May Her peace abide in you.
May Her presence illuminate your heart
Now and forever more.

May the blessings of God rest upon you,
May His peace abide in you.
May His presence illuminate your heart
Now and forever more.

We Shall Overcome

We shall overcome. We shall overcome.
We shall overcome some day.
Oh, deep in my heart, I do believe
we shall overcome some day.

We'll walk hand in hand.
We'll walk hand in hand.
We'll walk hand in hand some day.
Oh, deep in my heart, I do believe
we shall overcome some day.

We are not afraid.
We are not afraid.
We are not afraid today.
Oh, deep in my heart, I do believe
we shall overcome some day.

We shall in live peace.
We shall in live peace.
We shall in live peace some day.
Oh, deep in my heart, I do believe
we will live in peace some day.

Earth-Water-Fire-Air

The earth, the water, the fire, the air
return, return, return, return.
The earth, the water, the fire, the air
return, return, return, return.

Hey-hey hey-hey hey-hey hey-hey
Wo-wo wo-wo wo-wo wo-wo
Hey-hey hey-hey hey-hey hey-hey
Wo-wo wo-wo wo-wo wo-wo.

Rose, Rose, Rose

Rose, rose, rose, rose
let my heart bloom as the rose
that I may offer love's sweet fragrance
in this thy garden.
(Sing as a round.)

We Are One in the Spirit
We are one in the Spirit,
we are one in the Lord.
We are one in the Spirit,
we are one in the Lord.

And we pray that our unity
will this day be restored.
For we know we're God's children
by our love, by our love.
For we know we're God's children
by our love.

Thank you
Thank you for this (food), Lord
thank you for this (food).
This healing, this healing,
this healing (food).
(Repeat with "day," "friends," etc.)

'Tis a Gift to be Simple
'Tis a gift to be simple
'tis a gift to be free,
'tis a gift to come down
where we ought to be.

And when we have come down
to the place just right
we will be in the valley
of love and delight.

When true simplicity is gained
to bow and to bend
we won't be ashamed.
To turn and to turn
will be our delight
'til by turning and turning
we come round right.

Asalaam Aleikhum
Asalaam aleikhum aleikhum asalaam
Asalaam aleikhum aleikhum asalaam

RECOMMENDED READING

American Indians

Amoss, Pamela, *Coast Salish Spirit Dancing, The Survival of an Ancestral Religion*. University of Washington Press, 1978.

Brown, Joseph Epes, *The Sacred Pipe, Black Elk's Account of the Seven Rites of the Oglala Sioux*. University of Oklahoma Press, 1971.

McGaa, Ed, Eagle Man, *Mother Earth Spirituality, Native American Paths to Healing Ourselves and Our World*. Harper & Row, 1990.

Miller, Joaquin, *Life Amongst the Modocs: Unwritten History*. Urion Press, San Jose, 1987.

Powers, William K., *Sacred Language; The Nature of Super-natural Discourse in Lakota*. University of Oklahoma Press, 1986.

Powers, William K., *Yuwipi—Vision and Experience in Oglala Ritual*. University of Nebraska Press, 1982.

Waters, Frank, *The Book of the Hopi*. Viking Books, 1963.

Australian Aborigines

Lawlor, Robert, *Voices of the First Day—Awakening in the Aboriginal Dreamtime*. Inner Traditions, 1991.

Chakras and Color

Anderson, Mary, *Colour Healing*. The Aquarian Press, 1983.

Gardner, Joy, *Color and Crystals, A Journey Through the Chakras*. The Crossing Press, 1988.

Jones, Alex, *Seven Mansions of Color*. De Vorss & Co., 1982.

Holography and Physics

Talbot, Michael, *The Holographic Universe*. Harper-Collins, 1991.

India and Music

Massey, Reginald & Jamila, *The Music of India*. Kahn & Averill, 1976.

Matrilineal Societies

Briffault, Robert, *The Mothers*, Abridged by Gordon R.Taylor. Atheneum, 1977.

Eisler, Riane, *The Chalice & the Blade, Our History, Our Future*. Harper & Row, 1987.

Negro Spirituals

Thurman, Howard, *Deep River* and *The Negro Spiritual Speaks of Life and Death*. Friends United Press, 1975.

Tantra and Kundalini

Anand, Margo, *The Art of Sexual Ecstasy, The Path of Sacred Sexuality for Western Lovers*. Jeremy P. Tarcher, Inc., 1989.

Chang, Jolan, *The Tao of Love and Sex, The Ancient Chinese Way to Ecstasy*. E.P. Dutton, 1977.

Chia, Mantak and Maneewan Chia, *Healing Love Through the Tao, Cultivating Female Sexual Energy*. Healing Tao Books, 1986.

Chia, Mantak and Michael Winn, *Taoist Secrets of Love, Cultivating Male Sexual Energy*. Aurora Press, 1984.

Douglas, Nik and Penny Slinger, *Sexual Secrets, The Alchemy of Ecstasy*. Destiny Books, 1979.

Muir, Charles and Caroline, *Tantra, The Art of Conscious Loving*. Mercury House, Inc., 1989.

Sannella, Lee, M.D., *The Kundalini Experience—Psychosis or Transcendence?* Integral Publishing, 1987.

Vibrational and Holistic Health

Chopra, Deepak, M.D., *Quantum Healing, Exploring the Frontiers of Mind/Body Medicine*. Bantam Books, 1990.

Gerber, Richard, M.D., *Vibrational Medicine*. Bear & Co., 1988.

Gardner, Joy, *Color and Crystals, A Journey Through the Chakras*. The Crossing Press, 1988.

Gardner, Joy, *Healing Yourself During Pregnancy*. The Crossing Press, 1987.

Gardner, Joy, *The New Healing Yourself, Natural Remedies for Adults and Children*. The Crossing Press, 1989.

Hay, Louise, *You Can Heal Your Body*. Hay House, 1976.

Simonton, O. Carl, M.D., and Stephanie Matthews-Simonton, *Getting Well Again*. James Creighton, 1978.

Voice and Music for Healing

Andrews, Joel, *A Harp Full of Stars, The Journey of a Music Healer*. Golden Harp Press, P.O. Box 335, Ben Lomond, Ca. 95005.

Campbell, Don, editor, *Music Physician for Times to Come*. Quest Books, 1991.

Gardner, Kay, *Sounding the Inner Landscape, Music as Medicine*. Caduceus Publications, 1990.

Garfield, Laeh Maggie, *Sound Medicine*. Celestial Arts, 1987.

Keyes, Laurel Elizabeth, *Toning, The Creative Power of the Voice*. De Vorss, 1984.

Khan, Hazrat Inayat, *The Mysticism of Music Sound and Word, The Sufi Message*. Motilal Banarsidass, 1927.

Lasson, Chava, *Am I Laughing Too Loud?* Chava Lasson, 1034 12th St., #3, Santa Monica, Ca. 90403.

Lingerman, Hal A., *The Healing Energies of Music*. Quest Books, 1983.

CASSETTE TAPES AND COMPACT DISCS

Information

Healing Powers of Tone and Chant, a 2-cassette audio workshop.
  Healing with Tone and Chant by Don G. Campbell
  Chant: Healing Power of Voice & Ear presented byTim Wilson Quest Books, 1990.

The Roar of Silence by Don Campbell, Quest Books.

Solo & Group Overtone Chanting, an interview with Jill Purce. Available from 20 Willow Rd., London N.W. 3, 1984.

Sound Medicine by Laeh Maggie Garfield. Available from Inward Journeys, P.O. Box 1112, Ashland, Or. 97520.

Music, Chanting, Toning

Gandharva Veda Music, Vocal with Instrumental

Gregorian Chants (Dr. Tomatis recommends): Epiphany and Easter Mass, Dawn and Midnight Masses for Christmas, Masses of St. Stephen and St. Peter from The Abby of Solemnes

Enya: *The Celts, Watermark, Shepherd Moons*

Gardner, Joy, *The Healing Voice—Toning Meditations* available from Healing Yourself, P.O. Box 3414, Santa Cruz, Ca. 95063.

Gardner, Kay, *Sounding the Inner Landscape*

Hamill, Claire, *Voices*

Kaur, Singh, *Peace Lagoon*

Khan, Ali Akbar, *Master Musician, Morning and Evening Ragas*

McKennitt, Loreena, *The Visit*

Nakai, R. Carlos, *Desert Dance*

Sophia: *Hidden Waters & Sacred Ground, Journey Into Love*

Tallis, Thomas, *Renaissance Motets*

Thiel, Lisa, *Prayers for the Planet, Songs of Spirit East, Songs of Spirit West, Songs of Transformation*

Sabina, *Remember the Love*

CHAPTER REFERENCES

Chapter One

1. Khan, Hazrat Inayat, *The Mysticism of Music, Sound and Word, The Sufi Message, Volume II*. Motilal Banarsidass, Delhi, 1988, pp. 157-158.
2. Ibid, p. 182.
3. Chopra, Deepak, M.D., *Quantum Healing, Exploring the Frontiers of Mind/Body Medicine*. Bantam Books, New York, 1990, p. 18.
4. Chopra, Deepak, M.D., *Perfect Health, The Complete Mind/Body Guide*, Harmony Books, New York, 1990, pp. 131-133.
5. Waters, Frank, *The Book of the Hopi*, Penguin Books, New York, 1977, pp. 9, 5.
6. Powers, William K., *Sacred Language; The Nature of Super-natural Discourse in Lakota*. University of Oklahoma Press, Norman, Okla., 1986, p. 154.
7. Carpenter, Craig, in private conversation, June 1992.

Chapter Two

1. Talbot, Michael, *The Holographic Universe*. Harpins Collins, New York, 1991, pp. 14-18.

Chapter Three

1. Carpenter, Craig, in private conversation, June, 1992.
2. Powers, William K., *Sacred Language; The Nature of Super-natural Discourse in Lakota*. University of Oklahoma Press, Norman, Okla., 1986, p. 57.
3. Brown, Joseph Epes, *The Sacred Pipe, Black Elk's Account of the Seven Rites of the Oglala Sioux*. University of Oklahoma Press, Norman, Okla., 1971, p. 44.
4. Amoss, Pamela, *Coast Salish Spirit Dancing, The Survival of an Ancestral Religion*. University of Washington Press, Seattle, 1978, p. 52.
5. McGaa, Ed, Eagle Man, *Mother Earth Spirituality, Native American Paths to Healing Ourselves and Our World*. Harper & Row, San Francisco, Ca., 1990, pp. 61-72
6. Powers, 1986, p. 82.
7. Ibid, 1986, p. 70.
8. Brown, 1971, p. 45.
9. Amoss, 1978, p.13.
10. Powers, William K., *Yuwipi—Vision and Experience in Oglala Ritual*. University of Nebraska Press, Lincoln, Neb., 1982.
11. Dow, Mary Louise, with Wagenheim, Jeff, "Encounters with a Medicine Man." *New Age Journal*, July/August 1992: 48.
12. Powers, 1982, p. 60.
13. Ibid

14. Ibid, p. 70.
15. Dow, Mary Louise, 1992, pp. 118, 121.
16. Brown, 1971, p. 67-100.
17. Lawlor, Robert, *Voices of the First Day—Awakening in the Aboriginal Dreamtime.* Inner Traditions, Rochester, Vt., 1991, pp. 184-193.
18. Amoss, pp. 52-54, 142.
19. Ibid, pp. 25, 85, 53-55.
20. Ibid, pp. 161, 127-129.
21. Medley, Kathleen, in personal conversation, June 1992
22. Powers, 1986, p. 70.
23. Lawlor, 1991, p. 42.

Chapter Four

1. Lawlor, Robert, *Voices of the First Day—Awakening in the Aboriginal Dreamtime.* Inner Traditions, Rochester, Vt., 1991, p. 61.
2. Massey, Reginald & Jamila, *The Music of India.* Kahn & Averill, London, 1976, pp. 14-15.
3. Vander, Judith, *Ghost Dance Songs and Religion of a Wind River Shoshone Woman.* Monograph Series in Ethnomusicology, Number 4. The Regents of the University of California, 1986, p. 15.
4. Landsman, Yehuda, in private conversation, June, 1992.
5. Lawlor, 1991, p. 168.
6. Tatar, Elizabeth, *Nineteenth Century Hawaiian Chant.* Pacific Anthropological Records No. 33, March 1982, Department of Anthropology, Bernice P. Bishop Museum, Honolulu, Ha., pp. 18-25.
7. Kahananui, Dorothy M., *Music of Ancient Hawaii, A Brief Survey.* University of Hawaii, Honolulu, Ha., 1962, pp. 7, 15-16.
8. Tatar, 1982, pp. 19-21.
9. Carpenter, Craig, in personal conversation, March, 1990.

Chapter Five

1. Carpenter, Craig, in personal conversation, March, 1990.
2. Powers, William K., *Yuwipi—Vision and Experience in Oglala Ritual.* University of Nebraska Press, Lincoln, Neb., 1982.
3. Odum, Howard Washington and Johnson, Guy B., *The Negro and His Songs.* Folklore Associates, Inc., Hatboro, Pa., 1964, p. 34.
4. Tatar, Elizabeth, *Nineteenth Century Hawaiian Chant.* Pacific Anthropological Records No. 33, March 1982, Department of Anthropology, Bernice P. Bishop Museum, Honolulu, Ha., pp. 1-8, 24-28.
5. Thurman, Howard, *Deep River* and *The Negro Spiritual Speaks of Life and Death.* Friends United Press, Richmond, Ind., 1975, pp. 17-60.

6. Jacobs, Virginia Lee, *The Roots of Rastafari*, Avant Books, San Diego, Ca., 1985 (out of print), pp. 120-142.
7. Wilson, Tim "Chant: The Healing Power of Voice and Ear, An Interview with Alfred Tomatis, M.D.," *Music Physician for Times to Come, An Anthology* compiled by Don Campbell, Quest Books, Wheaton, Ill., 1991, p. 18.
8. Weeks, Bradford S., M.D., "The Physician, The Ear and Sacred Music," *Music Physician for Times to Come, An Anthology* compiled by Don Campbell, Quest Books, Wheaton, Ill., 1991, pp. 49-50, 39.
9. Carpenter, Craig, in personal communication, August, 1992.
10. McGaa, Ed, Eagle Man, *Mother Earth Spirituality, Native American Paths to Healing Ourselves and Our World.* Harper & Row, San Francisco, 1990, p. 89-90.

Chapter Six
1. Medley, Kathleen, in personal conversation, June 1992
2. Briffault, Robert, *The Mothers*, Abridged by Gordon Rattray Taylor. Atheneum, New York, N.Y., 1977.
3. Massey, Reginald & Jamila, *The Music of India.* Kahn & Averill, London, 1976, p. 26.
4. Lawlor, 1991, p. 226.
5. Lawlor, 1991, pp. 27-33.
6. Massey, 1976, p. 211.
7. Tayumanavar, Swami K.M., in private conversation, April 1992.
8. Lawlor, 1991, p. 180.
9. Muir, Charles, in Tantra Workshop on Maui, Hawaii, December, 1991.
10. Lewis, Dr. H. Spencer, *Sanctum Invocation and Vowel Intonations*, a cassette tape taken from record S-33, Rosicrucian Supply Bureau.

Chapter Seven
1. Wilson, Tim, "Chant: The Healing Power of Voice and Ear, An Interview with Alfred Tomatis, M.D.," *Music Physician for Times to Come, An Anthology* compiled by Don Campbell. Quest Books, Wheaton, Ill., 1991, pp. 27-28.
2. Miller, Clarence, D.Sc., *The Science of Musical Sounds.* The MacMillan Co., New York, 1916, p. 239.
3. Khan, Hazrat Inayat, *The Mysticism of Music, Sound and Word, The Sufi Message, Volume II.* Motilal Banarsidass, Delhi, 1988, p. 168.
4. Gardner, Joy, *Color and Crystals, A Journey Through the Chakras*, The Crossing Press, Freedom, Ca., 1988, pp. 139-141.

Chapter Eight
1. Hung, J.H. et al, *Fetal Diagnostic Therapy*, 1991; 6 (1-2): 65-73.

2. Scheppach, Joseph, "Ultrasound Sex," *Penthouse, The International Magazine for Men*, September 1992: 138-140.
3. Campbell, Don, *Music Physician for Times to Come, An Anthology*. Quest Books, Wheaton, Ill., 1991, p. 3.
4. Weeks, Bradford S., M.D., "The Physician, The Ear and Sacred Music," *Music Physician for Times to Come, An Anthology* compiled by Campbell, Don, Quest Books, Wheaton, Ill., 1991, p. 41.
5. Campbell, 1991, p. 3.
6. Wilson, Tim "Chant: The Healing Power of Voice and Ear, An Interview with Alfred Tomatis, M.D.," *Music Physician for Times to Come, An Anthology* compiled by Don Campbell. Quest Books, Wheaton, Ill., 1991, p. 13, 17.
7. Weeks, 1991, p. 40.
8. Wilson, pp. 19, 13-14.
9. Weeks, p. 47.
10. Wilson, pp. 18-21, 23.
11. Keyes, Laurel Elizabeth, *Toning, The Creative Power of the Voice*. DeVorss & Co., Marina del Rey, 1973, p. 99.
12. Information at shark exhibit at Monterrey Bay Aquarium in Monterey, California, November 1991.
13. Keyes, 1973, pp. 99-100.
14. Lynes, Barry, *Dr. Royal Rife, The Cancer Cure That Worked—50 Years of Suppression*. Marcus Books, Queensville, Ont., 1987.
15. Gardner, Kay, *Sounding the Inner Landscape, Music as Medicine*. Caduceus Publications, Stonington, Me., 1990, p. 29.
16. *The Varieties of Healing Experience: Exploring Psychic Phenomena in Healing*. Transcript of the interdisciplinary Symposium of October 30, 1971. Academy of Parapsychology and Medicine, Los Altos, Ca., 1973.
17. Cousins, Norman, *Anatomy of an Illness*. Bantam Books, New York, 1991, pp. 30-43.
18. Keyes, 1973, p. 108.

Chapter Nine
1. Garfield, Laeh Maggie, *Sound Medicine, Healing with Music, Voice and Song*. Celestial Arts, Berkeley. 1987, p. 57.
2. Lasson, Chava, *Am I Laughing Too Loud?*, Lasson, Santa Monica, Ca., 1989, pp. 35-36.

Chapter Ten
1. Selye, Hans, *Stress without Distress*. Lippincott, Philadelphia, 1974.
2. Simonton, O. Carl, M.D., *The Healing Journey*. Bantam, New York, 1992, pp. 4-5.
3. Hay, Louise, *You Can Heal Your Body*. Hay House, Santa Monica, Ca., 1976.

4. Hay, Louise, *AIDS: A Positive Approach/Healing*. Imagery tape. Hay House, Santa Monica, Ca.

5. Wilson, Tim "Chant: The Healing Power of Voice and Ear, An Interview with Alfred Tomatis, M.D.," *Music Physician for Times to Come, An Anthology* compiled by Don Campbell. Quest Books, Wheaton, Ill., 1991, pp. 19, 25.

6. Baer, Randall and Vicki, *The Crystal Connection*. Harper-Collins, New York, 1992.

Chapter Eleven

1. Tatar, Elizabeth, *Nineteenth Century Hawaiian Chant*. Pacific Anthropological Records No. 33, March 1982, Department of Anthropology, Bernice P. Bishop Museum, Honolulu, p. 37.

2. Odum, Howard Washington and Johnson, Guy B., *The Negro and His Songs*. Folklore Associates, Inc., Hatboro, Pa., 1964.

3. Landsman, Yehuda, in private conversation, June, 1992.

Chapter Twelve

1. Wilson, Tim, "Chant: The Healing Power of Voice and Ear, An Interview with Alfred Tomatis, M.D.," *Music Physician for Times to Come, An Anthology* compiled by Don Campbell. Quest Books, Wheaton, Ill., 1991, p. 22.

2. Gardner, Joy, *Healing Yourself During Pregnancy*. The Crossing Press, Freedom, Ca,. 1987, pp. 21-23, 56.

3. Purce, Jill, *Interview with Solo and Group Overtone Chanting*. Cassette tape available from 20 Willow Road, London N.W. 3, 1984.

4. Gardner, 1987, p. 153.

5. Rosenberg, Kurt, "Musically Midwifing Death," *Common Boundary*, September/October 1990.

6. Rose, Talia, in private conversation, August, 1992.

7. Vander, Judith, *Ghost Dance Songs and Religion of a Wind River Shoshone Woman*. Monograph Series in Ethnomusicology, Number 4. The Regents of the University of California, 1986, p. 64.

8. Amoss, Pamela, *Coast Salish Spirit Dancing, The Survival of an Ancestral Religion*. University of Washington Press, Seattle, 1978, p. 20.

9. Documentary of the Huichol Indians on PBS Television, 1992.

10. Transcript of Hopi Proceedings at Santa Fe, New Mexico, December 13, 1990, between Martin Gashweseoma and Governor-elect Bruce King. The Planting Stick Project, Route 9, Box 78, Santa Fe, N.M.

Toning Practitioners

Here is a short list of people who practice Toning for Healing. I have worked with and feel confident in the work of all of these people.

Celeste Crowley
37 View
Nelson, British Columbia V1L 2V3, Canada
(604) 352-1958

Celeste is a singer and musician who combines vocal work with Reiki (a form of laying-on-of-hands). She also uses sound work as a part of her Profound Clowning. She teaches workshops on "Experiencing Your Voice."

Ilianna Culver-Dufford, C.H.T.
1295-2 Piedmont Rd., Suite 25
San Jose, California 95132
(408) 259-4723

Ilianna uses a unique approach to the use of sound in healing by applying sound directly to the body, using her highly intuitive ability to determine the pitch and length of the sounds used. The result is a clearing of the mind and body of energetic blocks and making way for the infusion of higher frequency energies.

Joy Gardner-Gordon
P.O. Box 554
Woodacre, California 94973
(415) 488-9429

Joy works in Woodacre, near San Francisco, where she sees clients, teaches workshops on "The Healing Voice" and conducts a "Vibrational Healing Training Program" which includes toning. She also teaches internationally.

Laeh Maggie Garfield
P.O. Box 1112
Ashland, Oregon 97520
(503) 482-6630

Laeh Maggie Garfield, author of *Sound Medicine*, practices and teaches "Healing with Sound," introducing you to your Life Song and Healing Song. She also teaches toning and musical vitality.

Ruth Gould-Goodman, B.A., M.A.
1372 Appleton Way
Venice California 90291
(310) 392-3612

Ruth combines movement and dance therapy with toning in individual and group sessions. She is a licensed acupuncturist and a yoga teacher. She has been a teacher and a healing arts practitioner for twenty years.

Chava Lasson
1034 12th St. #3
Santa Monica, California 90403
(213) 395-8856

Chava has been teaching voice lessons for over sixty years, and combining this with Toning for over twenty. She does individual and group sessions.

"I work with the voice. I play with the voice. I do more with the voice than meets the word. I use voice to release tensions, heal the body, soothe the mind, express the soul and visage the future. Vibrations set into motion by the human sound go beyond the word to connect with deep deep meaning."

Center for Sound Healing, Patricia Lynn Mann, R.N., M.S.
P.O. Box 2157
Carmel Valley, California 93924
(408) 659-3031

Private sessions utilizing sound (toning, chanting) and energy work to transform body, mind and spirit. Workshops and group presentations on "Healing and Transformation Through Sound."

Sandia Rising Star
P.O. Box 1226
Middletown, California 95461
(707) 987-2228 or 869-0062

Sandia is a Dance Therapist who integrates toning, movement and ritual in a path of self exploration. She teaches "Healing Through Sound and Movement" and "The Dark Side of the Goddess." She lives near Harbin Hot Springs.

Talia Rose
P.O. Box 11896
San Raphael, California 94912
(415) 457-LOVE

Talia uses sound healing (voice and harp) as well as bodywork, conscious breathing and flower essences to help people dissolve old patterns and make transitions, including the final transition. This helps them to integrate their true vision and purpose. She teaches "Sound Healing."

TERMINOLOGY: AMERICAN INDIAN WORDS

cedar man—tends the fire and guards the entrances to the tepee at meetings of the Native American Church (see holy man).

grandfather—*tunkasila* in Lakota. Medicine men address all supernatural beings as Tunkasila, "Grandfather." For example, when they see the rainclouds gathering, they regard them as "thunder beings" and greet them as "Grandfather." This is an honorific term, and often the medicine or Yuwipi men or holy men will be addressed in this way. Sometimes stones that are used for the sweat will be addressed this way.

holy man (or woman) or priest—*wichasa wakan* in Lakota, is the one who performs ceremonies. Some white people call the holy man (or woman) who performs ceremonies a "medicine man." They say he is "making medicine" when he is performing ceremonies, but according to Sword, an Oglala Sioux, this is not accurate.

medicine—*pejuta* in Lakota. Something which is used to cure the sick or wounded. Among the Apache who are members of the Native American Church, peyote is called "medicine" and it is used literally as medicine, for various ailments, like any other herb. The people are very much opposed to using it for entertainment, like a drug. For them, it is both an herb and a sacrament. At peyote meetings, it is used in the context of a ritual.

medicine man (or woman) or Indian doctor—*pejuta wichasa* in Lakota is a person who cures the sick or wounded. This is usually a skill acquired originally through a vision.

Road Man: At peyote meetings, it is used in the context of a ritual. In this case, the man who leads the ritual is called the Road Man, because of the symbolic road that he draws in the sand at the beginning of the ceremony.

song—*syowen* in Coast Salish. The spirit helper that overpowers the Spirit Dancer and is expressed in the form of a song and dance.

sweat lodge—*inipi* in Lakota.

The following is an explanation of the intended meanings for some of the words commonly used in this book.

Terminology

alpha state : our common waking consciousness is at beta level which is 13 hertz and above. Alpha state of consciousness is 8-12 hertz which is a light state of relaxation that is very good for creative thinking, creative visualization and learning. Feelings of well being and euphoria are associated with the alpha state, probably due to the increase in the production of neuro-chemicals, beta endorphins, serotonin and norepinephrine.

beat is the regularly occurring amplification of sound produced by two simultaneous tones of nearly equal frequency.

chakras are spinning wheels of energy that are located along the spine. Most systems identify seven of these vortexes.

chant is a song or melody OR a simple liturgical (used in ritual or public worship) song in which a string of syllables or words is sung to each tone.

chromatic scale is the musical scale made up of thirteen successive half tones to the octave.

cochlea—see "ear."

consonant means harmonious in tone and refers to any speech sound produced by stopping and releasing the air stream (p, t, k, b, d, g), by stopping it at one point while it escapes at another (m,n,l,r), by forcing it through a loosely closed or very narrow passage (f,v,s,z,sh,zh,th,h, w, y) or by a combination of these means.

cult describes any system of religious worship or ritual, and it comes from the Latin *colere*, "to cultivate."

diatonic designates any standard major or minor scale of eight tones without the chromatic intervals.

droning is a bass voice sustaining a single low tone.

duration is the length of time that a sound is sustained.

ear, anatomical terms:
    cochlea is a snail-shaped canal in the inner ear
    vestibule is a central cavity of the labyrinth that makes up the inner ear
    external ear consists of the meatus and auditory canal
    middle ear consists of the tympanic membrane or eardrum, ossicles, middle ear muscles, oval and round window
    inner ear consists of the vestibular canal and cochlea
    stapedius muscle regulates the stapes, one of the three tiny bones (ossicles) of the middle ear; it is the only muscle in the human body that never rests.

electromagnetic spectrum is the complete range of frequencies of electromagnetic waves including, in order of increasing frequency: radio, microwaves, infrared, visible light, ultraviolet, X-ray, gamma ray, and cosmic ray waves. Only a small portion of these energies is visible: the seven-color spectrum of natural daylight. All radiation has the same velocity and the same electromagnetic nature; the only difference between parts of the spectrum are frequency and wave length. The range extends in frequency approximately from 10^{21} hertz to 0 hertz—or, in coresponding wavelengths, from 10^{-13} meter to infinity.

harmonic is the physical science dealing with musical sounds. Harmonics also pertain to overtones.

harmony is the simultaneous sounding of two or more tones, especially when satisfying to the ear. Harmony is the ratio and relationship between the tones and their rhythmic patterns.

hertz (hz) is a measure of the frequency of a sound wave; 1 hertz is equal to one cycle of sound waves per second.

idol is an image used as an object of worship, a false god, one that is the object of deep love or devotion.

idolatry is the worship of idols, blind admiration of or devotion to something or someone.

laser light is made by a device that contains a crystal (or some other suitable substance) which amplifies and concentrates light waves into an extremely pure form of visible light in which the amplitudes of wave patterns are perfectly aligned so that they rise and fall together. It emits a perfectly coherant light in a narrow, intense beam.

major scale is one of the two standard diatonic musical scales, with half steps instead of whole steps after the third and seventh tones.

melody is a sequence of single tones, usually in the same key or mode, to produce a rhythmic whole—often a tune, air, or song.

minor scale is one of the two standard diatonic musical scales, with half steps instead of whole steps after the second and seventh tones in ascending and after the sixth and third tones in descending (melodic minor scale) OR after the second, fifth, and seventh tones in ascending and after the eighth, sixth, and third tones in descending (harmonic minor scale) steps.

music is a combination of tone, rhythm and harmony.

noosphere is the atmosphere of ideas that surrounds the planet. This word was coined by Jesuit philosopher Teilhard de Chardin, who observed that new thoughts and concepts seem to enter the collective pool of ideas so that the same thought will arise at various places at the same time.

octave consists or eight notes and twelve semitones OR it is the eighth full note above a given tone, having twice as many vibrations per second, or below a given tone, having half as many vibrations per second. The Indian octave or *saptak* consists of seven notes and is divided into 22 intervals.

overtones are any of the higher tones heard with a fundamental tone, having a frequency of vibration that is an exact multiple of the frequency of the fundamental tone.

pitch is the number of vibrations per unit of time, which creates a low or high sound. Pitch refers to setting the key of the voice or a musical instrument in a particular vibrational frequency.

resonance is the reinforcement and prolongation of a sound or musical tone by reflection or by sympathetic vibration of other bodies.

rhythm gives definition, pattern and boundary to the tone. It can be a consistent repetitious beat or completely spontaneous, moving in and out of a beat pattern. With vocal sounds that are musical, rhythmic patterns can be constant, syncopated or completely chaotic.

scale is a series of tones arranged in a sequence of rising or falling pitches in accordance with any of various systems of intervals, especially all of such a series contained in one octave, including chromatic, diatonic and major scales.

song is a relatively short metrical composition for, or suitable for, singing, as a ballad or simple lyric.

stapedius see "ear".

syllable is a word or part of a word pronounced with a single, uninterrupted sounding of the voice; a unit of pronunciation, consisting of a single sound of great sonority (usually a vowel) and generally one or more sounds of lesser sonority (usually consonants).

timbre is the characteristic quality of sound that distinguishes one voice or instrument from another, which is determined by the harmonics of the sound and is distinguished from the volume and pitch.

tone is the utterance of a sound that is distinct and identifiable by its regularity of vibration, or constant pitch (as distinguished from a noise), and that may be put into harmonic relation with other such sounds.

tonic designates or is based on the first tone (keynote) of a diatonic scale.

toning (not defined in the current dictionary) is the use of sustained vocal tones, without the use of melody or rhythm, and without the use of words or specific meaning.

vestibule see "ear".

volume is the intensity of sound and the fullness of tone.

vowel is a voice speech sound characterized by generalized friction of the air passing in a continuous stream through the pharynx and opened mouth but with no constriction narrow enough to produce local friction; the sound of the greatest prominence in most syllables.

ABOUT THE AUTHOR

Joy Gardner-Gordon is a Vibrational Healer and a Life Path Counselor and the author of six books. She combines intuitive counseling and inner wisdom with ritual, toning, herbs and crystals. She has been a pioneer in the field of alternative health care and holistic health since 1970.

Also known as Joy Gardner, Ms. Gardner's books are internationally known. *Healing Yourself* appeared as the first modern medicinal herbal in 1972 and sold over 100,000 copies. It is now available in an updated and revised version, as *The New Healing Yourself*. Another book, *Color and Crystals*, was praised by *Yes! Books* in Arlington, Virginia: "We especially recommend it to those who are looking for practical information that they can apply to their own spiritual development."

Trained in western medicine as a women's paramedic, and licensed as a masseuse, Joy Gardner-Gordon has been working in the healing arts since 1970 as a Master Herbalist and a Women's Paramedic. She is the co-founder of The Siuslaw Rural Health Center in Oregon and the Nelson and District Hospice Society in British Columbia. She is a professional member of the American Herbalists Guild and the mother of two grown sons.

As a counselor, she studied death, loss and grief work with Swiss psychiatrist Elisabeth Kubler-Ross. Her gestalt skills were developed under the guidance of Bethal Phaigh, the author of *Gestalt and the Wisdom of the Kahunas*, who also taught her Reiki, a Japanese method of laying-on-of-hands. Having spent time among the Hopi, the Apache and other native people, her work and life philosophy are strongly influenced by their teachings.

In addition to her international recognition as an author, Ms. Gardner-Gordon has lectured at numerous universities, colleges, churches, EXPOs, herbal and midwifery schools and has appeared on TV and radio in the United States and Canada. Her diverse training and talents have enabled her to uncover and develop the unique and tremendously effective *Vibrational Healing* system she now teaches. Toning is an integral part of that system.

Joy Gardner-Gordon lives in Woodacre, California, near San Francisco where she sees clients, teaches workshops on *The Healing Voice* and conducts a Vibrational Healing Training Program. She travels internationally and is available for teaching engagements. She and her husband, Gordon, are currently writing a book about relationships, based on their counseling and group work with couples. For more information and to obtain Joy's cassette tape, *The Healing Voice—Toning Meditations*, write Vibrational Healing Program, P.O. Box 554, Woodacre, Ca. 94973 or call (415) 488-9429.

INDEX

A

Aborigines, Australian, 30, 31, 53, 164
  abortion, 55
  birth control, 55
  circumcision ritual, 15, 56
  Dreamtime, 16, 28, 54, 56, 57,
     153, 165
  sexual expression, 53
Abortion, Aborigine, 55
Adam and Eve, story of, 55
Aging as a result of poor breathing, 63. *See also* Senility
AIDS, toning for, 162
Alcohol, emotional release for, 99
Aloha spirit, 39–40
Alpha state of consciousness, 16, 31, 70
Alzheimer's Disease, use of sound for, 161
AMEIN as chart, 63
AMEN as chart, 63
American Indian. *See also* Shamanism
  chants, 167
  creation stories, 4
  doctor, 17, 25
  language, 57
Amoss, Pamela, 25
Angels, calling, 6
Anger, vision during, 24
Animal spirit helpers, 26
A-O-M
  as expression of power, 127
  expanded, 129, 166
Apache Indians, 9
Aphrodite, 53
Arthritis as a result of emotional repression, 103
Asthma, toning for, 63, 95
AUM as mantra, 71
Australian Aborigines. *See* Aborigines, Australian
Ayurvedic medicine, 4, 114

B

Baptist Church, 26

Bhagavad Gita, 30
Bible, 45, 55
Bird Dance Songs, Shoshone, 38
Birth control, herbal, 55
Black Elk, 19
Blood pressure
  effect of sound on, 81, 82
  high, emotional cause of, 104
Bodywork with toning, 96. *See also* Massage
Brain, effect of sound on, 125
Bray, Daddy, 32–42
Breathing. *See also* Diaphram
  effect of sound on, 81
  role of, in toning, 63
Bronchitis, toning for, 63
Brown, Joseph Epes, 19
Buddhism, toning in, 2, 12
Buffalo Calf Woman, 16
Bullroarers, role of, in circumcision, 56

C

Cancer, effect of sound on, 84
Cannibalism, 39
Cantor, 11
Car Noise Therapy, 104
Carpenter, Craig, 5, 16, 32–42
Catholic Church, 45
Ceres, 53
Cesarean delivery, 156
Chakras, 57, 112–128
  chart, 126
  definition of, 114
  list, 115117
  methods for opening, 147
  toning for, 125–127
Chanting. *See also* Sounding, Toning
  effect of, on heart, 82
  Gregorian, 82, 161
  overtone, 46, 47, 70
Chants, genealogy, 31
Childbirth. *See also* Pregnancy
  labor, 156–158

Toning. *See also* Sounding
  definition of, 1, 61
  in groups, 143
  methods of, 67
  session, 72
  where to do, 71
  with children, 72, 78
  with movement, 110
Traditionalists, 48, 58
Trance, 8, 9, 15, 23, 24, 26, 28, 55, 70
  as result of toning, 61
  and sixth chakra, 120
Tunkasila, 20

U
Ultrasound, 80

V
Vagus nerve, 81
Vedanta philosophy, 3
Venus, 53
Vibrational Alignment, 117–121, 138, 155, 156
Vibrational Healing, 83, 117
Vision Quest, 17–19, 24, 28
  sensory deprivation in, 16
Voice, releasing the, 106–110

W
Wailing, 2, 19, 23, 100, 120
Weeks, Dr. Bradford S., 47
Wohpekahmau, 16
Women, wild, 52
Women's rights, sexual and reproductive, 52
Words, power of, 3
Wovoka, 30

Y
Yab-yum position, 149–150
Yoga, 147
  Tantric, 57

Yoni, 54
Youngbear, Victor, 42
Youth
  respect for, 16
  grabbing of, in ritual, 25
Yurok, 16
Yuwipi, 44
  healing ritual, 20–22

Z
Zahlman, Rabbi Reb, 136
Zen. *See* Buddhism